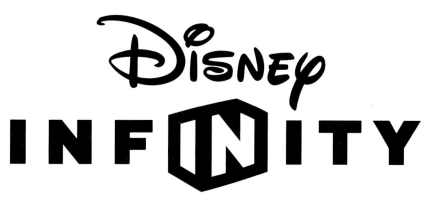

DISNEY INFINITY
PLAY WITHOUT LIMITS

CHARACTER ENCYCLOPEDIA

Written by **Catherine Saunders**

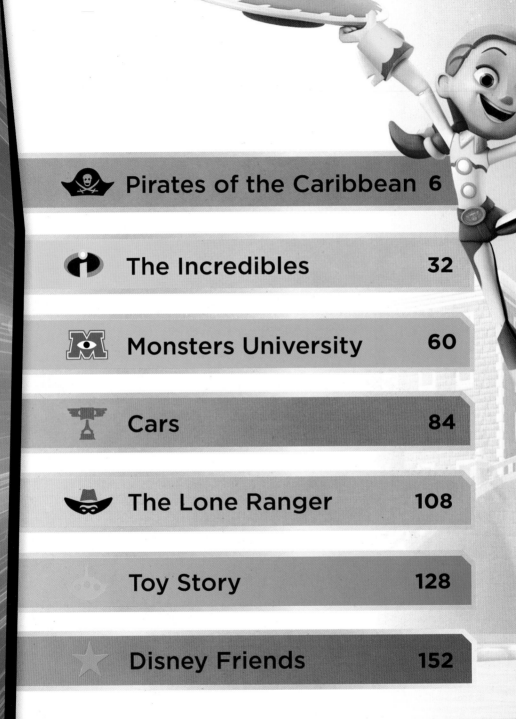

CONTENTS

INTRODUCTION

Welcome to the world of Disney Infinity. It's a crazy, mixed-up sort of place where anything might happen. You can search for pirate treasure or play monstrous pranks; maybe race around Radiator Springs or save a Wild West town. You can find out what it's like to have super powers or to visit Outer Space. Or how about having adventures with some feisty princesses or hanging out with some famous friends? But the best adventures will be the ones you invent yourself. So, go and unleash your imagination and have some fun!

PIRATES OF THE CARIBBEAN

Ahoy there land lubbers, here be pirates! It's an adventurous life, but a dangerous one. There is treasure aplenty, if you know where to find it, but beware of rough seas, scary monsters and worst of all, other pirates.

CONTENTS

CAPTAIN JACK SPARROW

Jack is the most famous pirate in the Caribbean. He has found – and lost – more treasure than he'd care to mention, but you can be sure that Captain Jack Sparrow is always ready for one more swashbuckling adventure.

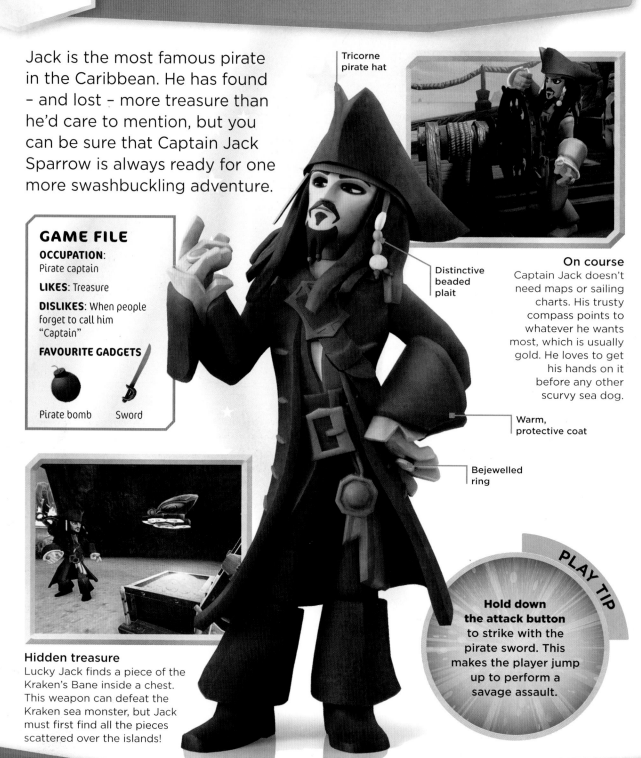

Tricorne pirate hat

GAME FILE

OCCUPATION:
Pirate captain

LIKES: Treasure

DISLIKES: When people forget to call him "Captain"

FAVOURITE GADGETS

Pirate bomb   Sword

Distinctive beaded plait

On course
Captain Jack doesn't need maps or sailing charts. His trusty compass points to whatever he wants most, which is usually gold. He loves to get his hands on it before any other scurvy sea dog.

Warm, protective coat

Bejewelled ring

Hidden treasure
Lucky Jack finds a piece of the Kraken's Bane inside a chest. This weapon can defeat the Kraken sea monster, but Jack must first find all the pieces scattered over the islands!

PLAY TIP
Hold down the attack button to strike with the pirate sword. This makes the player jump up to perform a savage assault.

BARBOSSA

Hector Barbossa is a cunning and daring sailor who has crossed the seven seas many times. Of course, Barbossa is also a pirate so he can't be trusted – just ask his old pal Captain Jack Sparrow about that!

Feather decorates wide-brimmed hat

GAME FILE

OCCUPATION: Pirate

WOULD LIKE TO BE: Captain of his own ship

FAVOURITE FRUIT: Apples

FAVOURITE ANIMALS: Monkeys

FAVOURITE GADGETS

Pirate bomb   Sword

Bushy brown hair

PLAY TIP

Once you complete the mission, A Captain Needs a Ship!, there's a cool new challenge for Barbossa **to defeat his enemies**, called Brawl at the Bay.

Sword belt

Fire!
Barbossa loves a good sea battle, especially when he is winning. A blast from his cannon will send his enemies scuttling back where they came from.

En garde
Barbossa has a habit of getting into fights. Fortunately, he's an expert swordsman with very fast reflexes. He is also a deadly shot with a flintlock pistol.

BUCCANEER BAY
AN EXCELLENT PIRATE HANGOUT

This important fort contains the Royal Navy's offices and also has a small jail. Jack knows it well!

Sturdy dinghies are great for sailing across town quickly – especially when Jack needs to rescue his crewmen!

Jack is on the lookout for a treasure chest that has been hidden up some rickety scaffolding.

It's a pirate's life for Jack Sparrow.

DAVY JONES

Heartless villain Davy Jones wasn't always so mean. He used to be a great pirate, famous for his daring exploits. Nowadays, though, he is part sea monster and has a reputation for being the scariest pirate on the high seas.

Barnacle-covered hat

PLAY TIP

To be a crack shot with the flintlock, **hold the aim button down** when facing an enemy. The pistol will lock on when the target is in range.

GAME FILE

ALIAS: Devil of the Seas

OCCUPATION: Pirate

ALLIES: The Kraken, Maccus

FAVOURITE GADGETS

Flintlock   Sword

Looking for trouble

Davy Jones will stop at nothing to defeat his enemies. Ready for action, he holds up a gleaming cutlass, as he races down the wharf.

Pirate sword

Monstrous pirate

Davy Jones has various sea monster parts, including tentacles and a crab claw for a hand. It's useful in the depths of the ocean – or for holding on to a clocktower!

Barnacle-covered wooden leg

MACCUS

Davy Jones' second-in-command is even less human than he is. Maccus resembles a huge walking, talking hammerhead shark, and he's got the scary personality to match. He will do anything his captain tells him, no matter how nasty.

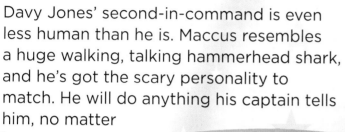

Scars from many battles

Face-off
Maccus' primary weapon is his formidable strength. However, he is large and slow, so he is susceptible to attacks from nimble swordsmen like Jack Sparrow.

Spikes on back

Lobster claw gauntlet

Night terror
On a dark night, it's best to steer clear of frightening foe Maccus. He has really sharp teeth, great eyesight and he can breathe underwater.

GAME FILE
OCCUPATION: Pirate/sea monster

FAVOURITE FOOD: Stingrays

SECRET: Maccus couldn't swim before he was turned into a sea monster.

PLAY TIP
In Schools of Fish to Fight, make sure you **put some distance between you and Maccus' crew** before opening fire. This will stop them from overwhelming you with an assault.

HOW TO SLAY A KRAKEN

MYSTICAL HELP AND PIRATE BLASTS

MISSION Find Tia Dalma
MISSION GIVER Gibbs

Captain Jack needs some advice. Mysterious Tia Dalma is as helpful as she is wise, but nobody knows where she lives. Jack has come to Pantano Bayou, but he needs help finding Tia Dalma.

1 Sail the dinghy up the river to Tia Dalma's house. Watch out for nasty turtles and debris.

MISSION Fightin' the Fish Faces
MISSION GIVER Pintel and Ragetti

Captain Jack must travel to Dead Man's Cove to find a missing piece of the Kraken's Bane. However, he is not alone – some of Davy Jones' crew are on the hunt, too.

1 After finding the cog, carefully open the door to the old fort. Watch out for Davy Jones' crew!

MISSION Last Piece Matey
MISSION GIVER Tia Dalma

The last piece of Kraken's Bane is somewhere in Buccaneer Bay, but Davy Jones' crew are also after this weapon. Captain Jack will have to fight them all!

1 Throwing some bombs or using the Atlas Blade should deal with the first group of enemies.

2

Dock the dinghy, but get ready for more enemy attacks. Defeat them with a cool combo move.

3

Use the compass to locate the ladder that leads to Tia Dalma's house. Let's hope she's at home!

TIA DALMA FOUND

2

The cursed crew are looking for a fight – a few bombs in their direction should slow them down.

3

Keep using the bombs to push back the pirates, but be ready for close combat, too.

200 COINS EARNED

2

Maccus the pirate won't give up easily. It'll take a shot from the blunderbuss to defeat him.

3

If Captain Jack wins the battle, he will find the last piece of Kraken's Bane inside the tower's bell.

1,000 COINS EARNED

GIBBS

Joshamee Gibbs is Jack Sparrow's first mate, which means he is his second-in-command. Gibbs has rescued his captain many times and he is as dependable and loyal as any pirate. However, that's not saying much: Gibbs once left Jack stranded on a desert island!

Short, grey hair

Beast from the deep
Gibbs is an experienced sailor and always keeps his eyes peeled for the Kraken sea monster. But sometimes this scary beast wraps its long tentacles around the ship faster than Gibbs can raise the alarm!

Distinctive sideburns

GAME FILE

OCCUPATION: Pirate

LIVES BY:
The Pirate's Code

LIKES: A few tankards of grog every now and then

DISLIKES: Getting caught

Stylish pirate belt and sash

Up on deck
Gibbs likes to survey the horizon for rival pirate ships from the top deck. He can also keep an eye on the rest of his scurvy crewmen, too!

PLAY TIP

Take part in Gibbs' missions and **you will find a ship** to help you reach Tia Dalma on her island. Helpful Gibbs will also teach you how to navigate the island.

TIA DALMA

Magical and mysterious Tia Dalma is a powerful and clever woman. In fact, she used to be a sea goddess named Calypso until Davy Jones tricked her into becoming human. Tia is still pretty cross about that and wants to get her revenge.

Dreadlock hairstyle

PLAY TIP

One of Tia's missions involves fighting a gang of pirates on their ship. Try **fighting them at the front of the ship** – they have fewer cannons there.

Magical pendant

Mystical charms

Powerful ally
Tia will gladly help out her old friend Jack Sparrow to collect all the pieces of the Kraken's Bane. She gives him tips on the trail and warns him about scary enemies he will have to fight.

Home sweet home
Tia lives on an island called Pantano Bayou. It's only a short distance by boat from Buccaneer Bay, but many dangers lurk in the swampy bayou surrounding Tia's house.

GAME FILE

ALSO KNOWN AS: Calypso

OCCUPATION: Sorceress

LIKES: Helping people, except Davy Jones

DISLIKES: Davy Jones

TOY BOX
PIRATE GRAND PRIX

Davy Jones has roamed the sea and land looking for friends to race around Port Royal. He knows that the best adventures happen when his crew comes along for the ride. With this lot joining him anything can happen!

This beach ball has a habit of turning up in a lot of adventures, but no one knows who it belongs to!

Violet is a little nervous – she hasn't passed her driving test yet!

Davy has borrowed this race track from his pal Ralph. He thinks it's just what Port Royal has been missing.

PLAY TIP

Take time to **explore the Toy Box Launch mode surroundings** when playing in this mode for the first time. Then begin building your own amazing world.

Lightning McQueen is in last place, but he is about to perform a daring overtaking manoeuvre.

Davy Jones is cheating, of course. He's stolen Merida's horse, Angus.

PINTEL

Pintel is one of the worst pirates in the Caribbean – and not in a fierce way. He has a special talent for finding curses, being taken prisoner and generally picking the wrong side in a battle. Luckily, he usually has his nephew Ragetti to keep him company.

Shiny bald head

Grubby neckerchief

GAME FILE

OCCUPATION: Pirate

LIKES: Gold

DISLIKES: Not having any gold

MOST LIKELY TO: End up in jail

Helping hand
Pintel and Ragetti are sometimes actually of some use. They are able to help Captain Jack find Gibbs and free him.

Ragged jacket

Trying hard
Pintel loves being a pirate and he especially enjoys a good fight. He will lead Captain Jack to Davy Jones' crew and help Jack blast them with pirate bombs.

PLAY TIP

It might not seem like a good idea, but **follow Pintel and Ragetti** in the We Know Where Gibbs Be mission. They know exactly where he is and will help you to find him.

RAGETTI

One-eyed pirate Ragetti looks pretty fearsome. However, when it comes to brains he's a few galleons short of a fleet. He can barely find his false eye, let alone any treasure. Along with his hapless Uncle Pintel, Ragetti has a knack for getting into trouble.

Wooden eye

Golden earring

PLAY TIP

In the Another Piece Be Here mission from Pintel and Ragetti, the goal is to get to the top of the moving platforms. Take your time and **let the platforms line up.**

GAME FILE

OCCUPATION: Pirate

DISTINGUISHING FEATURES:
A wooden eye

MOST LIKELY TO: Have no idea what's going on

LEAST LIKELY TO:
Win a talent contest

Admiring the view
Dopey Ragetti never knows what is going on. While Jack throws a Pirate Bomb to blow open the locked gate at Dead Man's Cove, Ragetti just stands back to admire the pretty fireworks!

Ill-fitting trousers

Deck shoes

Hasty escape
Ragetti is not the smartest pirate – he takes after his uncle. Whenever they find themselves in danger, they do the most obvious thing and start running!

If Captain Jack's ship cannot sail close enough to a place, he heads out to investigate in his dinghy.

There are many enticing islands and rocky coves, but it's not always easy to reach them – the seas are treacherous.

This ragged galleon hardly looks like it is seaworthy, but it has been part of many exciting adventures.

Barbossa spies treasure, ahoy!

DRIFTWOOD

This terrifying member of Davy Jones's crew used to be human, but now he looks like a wreck – a shipwreck. His body is made of slimy, rotten driftwood, the kind you find lurking at the bottom of the ocean. Watch out – if you get too close, he might give you a splinter!

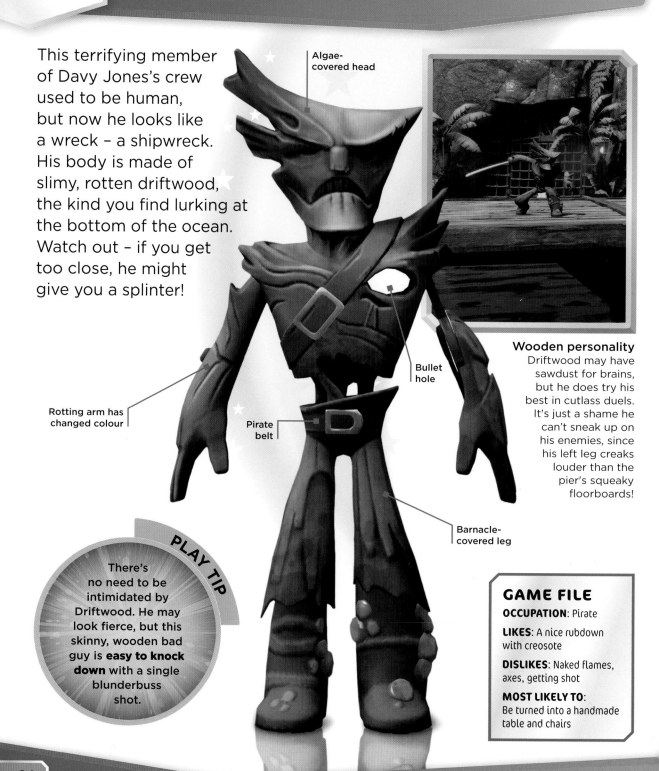

Algae-covered head

Bullet hole

Rotting arm has changed colour

Pirate belt

Barnacle-covered leg

Wooden personality
Driftwood may have sawdust for brains, but he does try his best in cutlass duels. It's just a shame he can't sneak up on his enemies, since his left leg creaks louder than the pier's squeaky floorboards!

PLAY TIP
There's no need to be intimidated by Driftwood. He may look fierce, but this skinny, wooden bad guy is **easy to knock down** with a single blunderbuss shot.

GAME FILE

OCCUPATION: Pirate

LIKES: A nice rubdown with creosote

DISLIKES: Naked flames, axes, getting shot

MOST LIKELY TO: Be turned into a handmade table and chairs

CLAM

This nautical bad guy always puts himself first – he is just really "shellfish". He packs a mean punch and his tough body can withstand most attacks. However, underneath his hard exterior, Clam has a soft centre. At times, he wishes that people would dig deeper and get to know the real him!

GAME FILE

OCCUPATION: Pirate

PERSONALITY: Tough guy with a hidden sensitive core

FAVOURITE FOOD: Plankton

DON'T MENTION: Clam chowder – he has nightmares about it

Sharp spike

Bulging biceps muscle

Shell-armoured body

Protective gauntlet

Stay back, Jack!
Clam always follows the orders of his captain, Davy Jones, especially if they are to fight Captain Jack. Clam favours a leaping attack style, that makes use of his deadly range and long sword.

PLAY TIP

Clam will try to block your attack. Wait until he comes near, **block his attack**, and then take him by surprise with a swift counterattack.

SWORD

Captain Jack never knows when he'll need to fight off a naval officer, a rival pirate or a sea monster, so he always keeps his cutlass handy.

Razor-sharp cutlass blade

Jack's compass

Bomb with quick-burning fuse

Lantern to help spot enemies

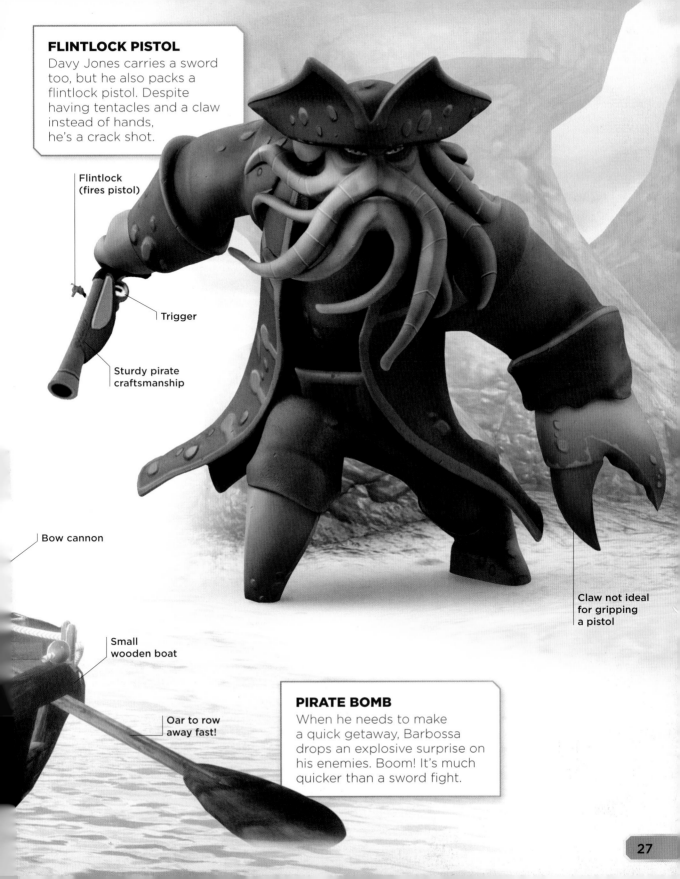

FLINTLOCK PISTOL
Davy Jones carries a sword too, but he also packs a flintlock pistol. Despite having tentacles and a claw instead of hands, he's a crack shot.

Flintlock
(fires pistol)

Trigger

Sturdy pirate
craftsmanship

Bow cannon

Claw not ideal
for gripping
a pistol

Small
wooden boat

Oar to row
away fast!

PIRATE BOMB
When he needs to make a quick getaway, Barbossa drops an explosive surprise on his enemies. Boom! It's much quicker than a sword fight.

PIRATES VS ROBOTS

Pirates don't have many friends – roguish treasure-seekers don't make reliable pals. But when Captain Jack, Barbossa and Davy Jones come up against some Zurgbots, they realise that they must work as a team to defeat them.

Captain Jack hopes that a hearty speech will convince the Zurgbots to depart peacefully.

Davy Jones is wielding a goo grower, and he won't hesitate to use it!

PLAY TIP

Focus on defeating the foes who are throwing pirate bombs in the Davy Jones Collects Souls Adventure, as these enemies cause the most trouble.

HELPING A FRIEND IN NEED

HUNT FOR MAGICAL ARTIFACTS AND TREASURE

MISSION Lost Me Some Light
MISSION GIVER Tia Dalma

Tia Dalma's hut is dark and gloomy, but the powerful ore of light would solve the problem. Find the five pieces of the ore to shed a little light for Tia Dalma.

1 Jump up on top of her house and try to find the first piece, then leap back down to collect the second.

MISSION You Wan' Magic? So Do I
MISSION GIVER Tia Dalma

Be careful – this is a very dangerous mission! Tia Dalma has lost her powerful magic rune. She is desperate to find it before it falls into the wrong hands.

1 Tia Dalma says the rune can be found on Port Talon Island. Meet her at the entrance of a cave there.

MISSION Find Some Shine
MISSION GIVER Tia Dalma

There's a rumour going round Port Royal that there is treasure to be had in Dead Man's Cove. But who would be brave enough to sail the stormy seas and seek it out? Captain Jack, of course!

1 It seems that the treasure chest is easy to find. Don't relax now – it could be a trick, of course!

2 The third piece is balanced on the end of a branch. Check the right side of the house to find the fourth.

3 Head to the top of the tree house to find the final piece. It is on a platform just above the roof.

200 COINS EARNED

2 Find the bonfire in the cave. Blow it up and open the chest you find there, automatically locking the gates.

3 Locate the magic rune and fight off the three pirates who will try to take it away.

500 COINS EARNED

2 Touching the chest locks the gates and activates some bloodthirsty pirates. Defeat the pirates to claim the treasure.

1,000 COINS EARNED

THE INCREDIBLES

Come and pay a visit to Metroville. This beautiful city is built on three islands: Small Island, Big Island and Headquarters. Surrounded by water on all sides, Metroville is a peaceful, safe, happy place – most of the time!

CONTENTS

Mr Incredible is the strongest super hero on the planet and he is dedicated to making the world a safe place to live. Good people can relax when he's around, but bad people had better watch out...

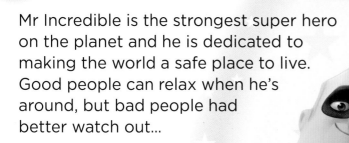

Super strength
Mr Incredible packs a hefty punch and he can toss an Omnidroid away like it was a sweet wrapper. No villain is a match for him.

GAME FILE

ALIAS: Bob Parr

LIKES: Saving people

DISLIKES: Paperwork

WORRIES: If he'll fit into his Super suit

FAVOURITE GADGETS

Incredicar   Glider

Super suit

Protective gloves

Burning rubber
There may be sparks and billowing smoke, but this Super keeps his cool. His sports car's reinforced chassis can withstand the mightiest of explosions.

PLAY TIP

Hold down the attack button to see Mr Incredible perform a powerful **uppercut punch combo.** It's enough to make his enemies see stars.

It is not easy keeping a family of super heroes out of trouble, but Mrs Incredible is extremely versatile. This flexible super hero can tie a bad guy in knots while still making sure that her kids do their homework.

Mask to conceal identity

Bendy body
Extra flexible Mrs Incredible can easily stretch her body like elastic and mould and twist it into virtually any shape. Dodging bullets is no problem for this bendy super hero.

GAME FILE

ALIASES: Helen Parr

LIKES: Keeping everyone safe

DISLIKES: Secrets

SPECIAL ABILITY: She can stretch her body until it's only 1mm thin.

FAVOURITE GADGETS

Incredicar   Hover board

Special super-stretchy suit

Long black boots

PLAY TIP

Before attempting a jump with the hover board, **allow it to ride** into the air for a little while. A hasty jump can cause a nasty fall.

High-kicking heroine
Mrs Incredible can unleash a powerful high kick on an unsuspecting Omnidroid before it knows what's hit it! She's skilled at keeping multiple attacking bad guys at bay.

MISSION The Secret of Heroes Island
MISSION GIVER Edna Mode

Syndrome has attacked the Supers' headquarters on Heroes Island and destroyed a bridge. The Incredibles need to get the base running again as soon as possible.

1 Buy a new bridge from the Toy Store to replace the destroyed one. Cross it and head for the Hall of Heroes.

MISSION Science to the Rescue
MISSION GIVER Mirage

A science agent has hidden a powerful weapon in the city. Syndrome wants to get his evil hands on it. Mr Incredible must protect it from the super villain.

1 Pick up the science agent in a car and take him through the city to the weapon.

MISSION The Final Showdown
MISSION GIVER Cop

It is time to defeat Syndrome once and for all. Mr Incredible has tracked him to the top of a building and leaped across to face him. Let battle commence!

1 Run back and forth along the rooftop to dodge Syndrome's powerful purple energy balls.

500 COINS EARNED

2

Climb the side of the building and find golden buttons to reactivate the HQ.

3

Aim to reach the centre spot at the top of the HQ in order to complete the mission.

100 COINS EARNED

2

The scientist activates the weapon, and Omnidroids try to get it. Fight them off before they damage it.

3

Use one Omnidroid to push over the others. Protect the weapon until it is ready to launch.

2,500 COINS EARNED

2

Syndrome launches Omnidroids at you. Throw them back at him and his rocket-launching droids.

3

Avoid the Omnidroid Tanks' lasers and destroy them. Beat Syndrome by hurling a robot at him.

DASH INCREDIBLE

Dash is the fastest kid in school, if only his parents would let him show it. At least when he's helping his family fight villains, Dash can use his talents. Most bad guys never even see this speedy little guy coming!

Road race
Dash thinks he's the fastest thing on the planet, but Lightning McQueen disagrees. It's time these two put their speed to the test – the race is on!

Slicked-back hair

Protective gloves

Incredibles logo

Holding on!
Dash loves being a super hero, but sometimes it can be a dangerous job. Fortunately, one of his Super family is usually on hand to rescue him.

GAME FILE

FULL NAME: Dashiell Robert Parr

PERSONALITY: Confident and brave

FAVOURITE GADGETS

Hover board

Incredicopter

PLAY TIP
Super speedy Dash may be an ace driver and awesome pilot, but he's usually **fastest on his own two feet**. They don't call him Dash for nothing!

VIOLET INCREDIBLE

Violet looks like a typical moody teenager, but she has much bigger problems than her classmates. She is just learning to deal with her amazing superpowers and coming to terms with being part of an Incredible family.

Long, straight hair

Mask means nobody recognises her – even her schoolmates!

PLAY TIP

Unlock the HQ and look out for kung-fu trainer. This will allow Violet to find out about her core abilities. It's sure to give her an edge over her enemies.

Black protective boots

Tumbling trick
Violet can turn invisible whenever she doesn't want to be seen – but that's not much help when she's standing in the path of an Omnidroid missile. Luckily, she can cartwheel away from danger, too!

GAME FILE
NICKNAME: Vi
PERSONALITY TYPE: Painfully shy
SECRET CRUSH: Tony Rydinger
FAVOURITE GADGETS

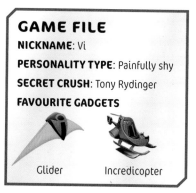

Glider   Incredicopter

Powerful force
Violet is very shy and quiet, except when it comes to protecting others. She can create a big defensive force field or blast smaller force fields at her enemies.

THE HEART OF METROVILLE

A PLACE THE INCREDIBLES CALL HOME

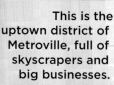

This emergency water tank on top of a building comes in handy if one of the Supers needs to put out a fire.

This is the uptown district of Metroville, full of skyscrapers and big businesses.

Many of the skyscrapers have flat roofs, like this one. They are the ideal landing spot for the Incredicopter.

Mrs Incredible is at the top of her game!

SYNDROME

Superfan Buddy Pine dreamed of becoming Mr Incredible's sidekick, but the Super rejected him. Buddy was very disappointed and decided to become a villain instead. He changed his name to Syndrome and swore to defeat his former hero!

Back-combed hair looks like flames

Evil genius
Syndrome might not be a Super, but he is smart. He has used his brains to become the most evil villain in Metroville, with an army of terrifying Omnidroids to carry out his wicked plans.

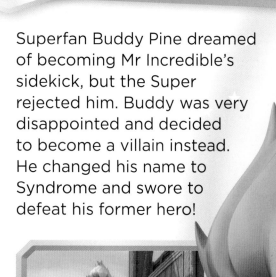

Gadget master
Thanks to his rocket boots, Syndrome can fly. He has also developed a Zero Point Energy device that allows him to hurl his enemies around. He is nearly as strong as Mr Incredible now!

Swishy super villain cape

Spotless white rocket boots

GAME FILE
REAL NAME: Buddy Pine
OCCUPATION: Super villain
NEMESIS: Mr Incredible
FATAL FLAW: Overconfidence
FAVOURITE GADGETS

Zero Point Energy gauntlet   Glider

PLAY TIP

Take care on rooftop conveyor belts in Syndrome's Sorting Sprint mission. If you fall off the roof, you will be transported back up, but it will waste precious time.

RICK DICKER

Grey-suited Rick Dicker works for the National Supers Agency, or NSA, an organisation that helps super heroes. He is assigned to the Incredibles and the danger-loving family keeps him very busy. Over the years though, he has grown very fond of them all.

Sensible haircut

GAME FILE
OCCUPATION: NSA agent

LIVES: Metroville

INTERESTS: None, he is too busy working

TOP SECRET: He would love a ride on Mrs Incredible's hover board.

No-nonsense expression

Boring, grey business suit

Skilled operative
Rick has perfected the art of looking ordinary and not drawing attention to himself, just like his suited NSA colleagues. He wishes Mr Incredible could do the same!

PLAY TIP
Save Metroville from doom in Rick's Bomb Scare mission. Locate the bombs and then **immerse them in water** to destroy them.

Tough job
Rick Dicker helps heroes like Mr Incredible to create believable cover stories and also coordinates their risky missions. If a Super makes a mistake, it means a lot of paperwork for him.

TOY BOX
AMAZING ADVENTURE

Syndrome is no match for Dash and his pal Agent P. The clever twosome has lured the over-confident villain and his Omnidroids into a maze and now they can't work out how to get out. Not feeling quite so smart now, are you Syndrome?

Syndrome is starting to feel really frustrated. He is an evil genius – surely he can work his way out of a stupid maze!

PLAY TIP

There are various capsules in the Toy Box Launch that will help you along the way. **Try touching the blue capsules** to get tips and information about the game.

The maze is constructed from simple blocks, which can be rearranged into new designs.

This hulking Omnidroid is too dim to work out that he could probably just stomp his way out of the maze.

Agent P is an expert at finding his way around mazes. He can solve them in seconds, unlike Syndrome.

Dash proves that he's clever as well as speedy. He's outwitted Syndrome without breaking a sweat.

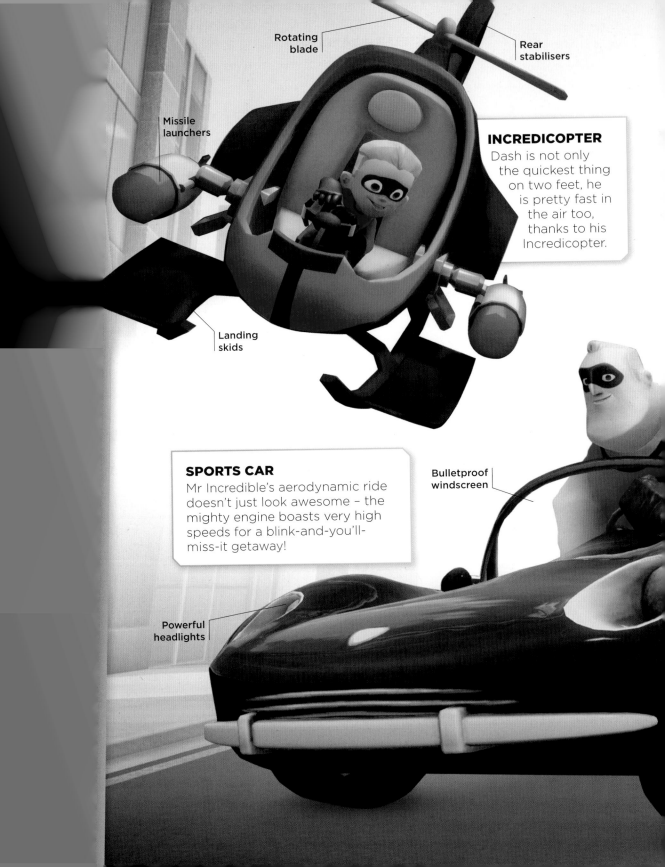

Rotating blade

Rear stabilisers

Missile launchers

INCREDICOPTER
Dash is not only the quickest thing on two feet, he is pretty fast in the air too, thanks to his Incredicopter.

Landing skids

SPORTS CAR
Mr Incredible's aerodynamic ride doesn't just look awesome – the mighty engine boasts very high speeds for a blink-and-you'll-miss-it getaway!

Bulletproof windscreen

Powerful headlights

HOVER BOARD

When she needs to get somewhere in a hurry, Mrs Incredible leaps onto her hover board. It is small, stylish and incredibly fast.

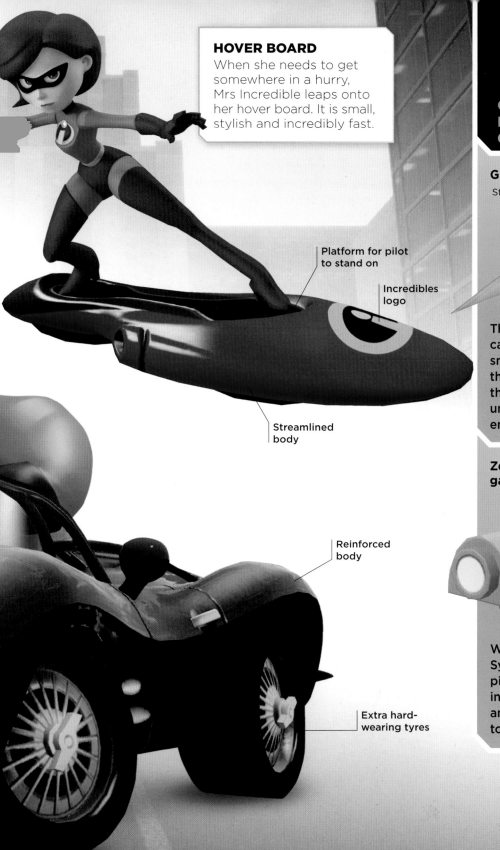

Platform for pilot to stand on

Incredibles logo

Streamlined body

Reinforced body

Extra hard-wearing tyres

Glider

Straps attach to body of glide pack

This graceful glider carries its passengers smoothly through the skies, helping them to swoop on unsuspecting enemies.

Zero Point Energy gauntlet

Super static charger

With this device, Syndrome can pick up objects – including people and vehicles – and toss them around.

EDNA MODE

She may be small, but there's nothing tiny about Edna Mode's talent. She is a fashion genius with impeccable taste and her speciality is designing super hero costumes. Edna, or E to her friends, only has one golden rule – no capes, dahling.

Super helper
Edna arrives in Metroville in her sleek helicopter to meet Mr Incredible. She definitely knows how to travel in style! Edna's here to help the Incredibles prepare for their missions, and give clues along the way.

Poker-straight bob

Stylish glasses

Practical but elegant dress

GAME FILE

OCCUPATION: Fashion designer

FRIENDS: The Incredibles

ENEMIES: Syndrome, anyone who wears a cape

MOST LIKELY TO SAY: Dahling, don't tell me what is impossible!

PLAY TIP

Complete Edna's A Shop of Her Own mission to stop Syndrome's Zero Point Energy weapon working on you. It is a quick way to get ahead in the game.

MIRAGE

Brainy, elegant Mirage used to be Syndrome's right-hand woman, helping him carry out his evil plans. However, when she met the Incredibles, she realised that she didn't want to be a baddie anymore and switched sides. Nowadays, Mirage works at the Incredibles headquarters instead.

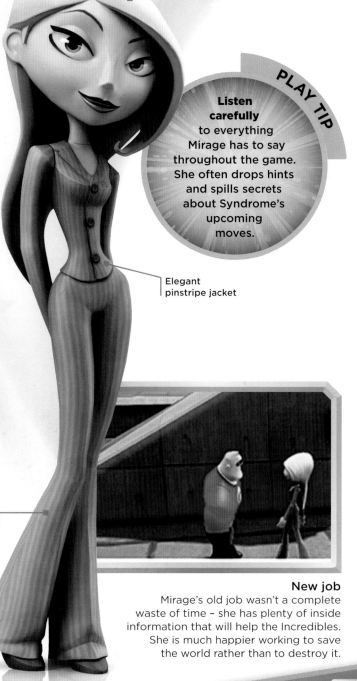

Ice-blonde hair

PLAY TIP

Listen carefully to everything Mirage has to say throughout the game. She often drops hints and spills secrets about Syndrome's upcoming moves.

Elegant pinstripe jacket

Matching trousers

Old job
At first, Mirage enjoyed working for Syndrome – he has a brilliant mind, albeit an evil one. Soon she realised that Syndrome was dangerous, and had to be stopped before he created chaos.

GAME FILE
OCCUPATION: Personal assistant

PERSONALITY TYPE:
Calm under pressure

DISLIKES: Realising your boss is a power-crazed super villain

LIKES: Being on the right side

New job
Mirage's old job wasn't a complete waste of time – she has plenty of inside information that will help the Incredibles. She is much happier working to save the world rather than to destroy it.

The swinging cranes that tower over the docks make fast getaways a little tricky. Luckily, Violet can dodge and duck under them in the Incredicopter!

The docks are situated near the Downtown business district. Mr Incredible's business is to keep them secure from danger.

These big crates hold cargo, but they also also act as platforms to run across when a Super is busy with a rescue.

Hold on - Mr Incredible is on his way!

ARMY OF OMNIDROIDS

An army of scary Omnidroids has been created by Syndrome, as part of his evil plan to take over the city of Metroville and destroy the Incredibles. The Omnidroids are formidable opponents and have been programmed to carry out his wicked orders. Watch out, Supers!

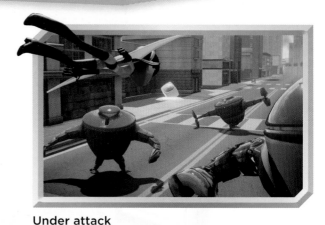

Under attack
Violet is outnumbered by the Omnidroids, but she's not scared – she's an Incredible! She glides over the tough machines and proves that they are no match for her.

GAME FILE

INVENTED BY: Syndrome

PROGRAMMED TO: Create chaos and destruction

LOYALTY: None – they are machines

Visual sensors

Flamethrower

Omnidroid #1
This variant is armed with homing missiles and flamethrowers, which are ideal for close-range attacks.

When faced with an army of Omnidroids, try picking up objects, such as cars, and **toss them at the Omnidroids**. It's a clever defence strategy.

Aerial assault
Dash is sure he could outrun the Omnidroids, but he thinks it will be fun to use his Incredicopter instead. They may be heavily armed, but the hulking robots can't fly.

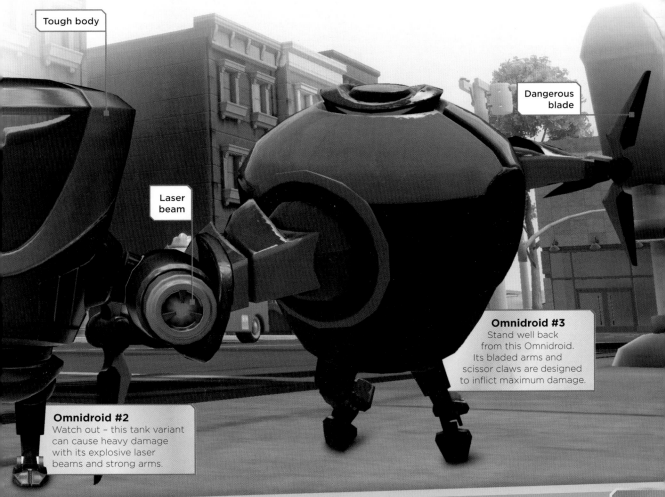

Tough body

Laser beam

Dangerous blade

Omnidroid #3
Stand well back from this Omnidroid. Its bladed arms and scissor claws are designed to inflict maximum damage.

Omnidroid #2
Watch out – this tank variant can cause heavy damage with its explosive laser beams and strong arms.

TOY BOX
CANDY TIME

Sometimes heroes need to take a break from saving the world and hang out with their buddies. Mr Incredible, Sulley, the Lone Ranger and Woody were enjoying their time out in a candy-themed land, until they found themselves in a sticky situation....

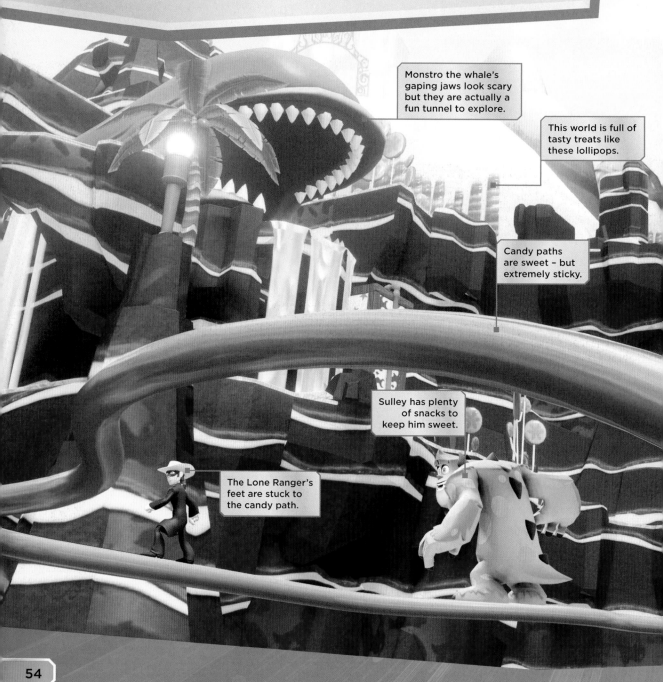

Monstro the whale's gaping jaws look scary but they are actually a fun tunnel to explore.

This world is full of tasty treats like these lollipops.

Candy paths are sweet – but extremely sticky.

Sulley has plenty of snacks to keep him sweet.

The Lone Ranger's feet are stuck to the candy path.

PLAY TIP

In Mr Incredible's The Hero Adventure, **focus on knocking down the domes** rather than destroying the enemies. You only score when you hit the domes.

Mr Incredible could break up the path, but it's a long way down....

Woody wishes he could fly, like his pal Buzz.

METROVILLE CITIZENS

Metroville City is made up of three islands and is home to thousands of different citizens. Some work hard to keep the city's businesses thriving, while others strive to keep the roads running smoothly. Most live quiet, simple lives, wanting nothing more than to keep their family and friends safe and happy. Come and meet some of them.

GAME FILE

SMALL ISLAND: This residential district houses schools and hospitals.

BIG ISLAND: Also known as the Metroville Business District

HEADQUARTERS: The premier training facility in town, the NSA Headquarters has given Metroville some of its best super agents.

Hardworking teacher
Metroville prides itself on its top-quality education system. This Metroville resident teaches history and art.

Sensible haircut

Trendy quiff

Working mum
This busy mum thinks that Metroville is a great place to raise her family. It's so peaceful and safe.

Funky earrings

Student
This student loves the ocean, so he is studying marine biology at Metroville University.

PLAY TIP

Fling the citizens off the top of buildings – it's the quickest way to get them to safety in Mrs Incredible's Grab-It mission. Don't worry – they use parachutes to float down safely.

City under attack

The people of Metroville are about to get a nasty shock. Syndrome doesn't care about the city, or its citizens. He will even pick them up and throw them onto rooftops like playthings, in order to get points!

Protective hard hat

Maintenance man

The roads in Metroville are in great shape, thanks to this guy. If any potholes appear, he'll fix them right away.

Thick glasses

Incredible rescue

Mr Incredible's chunky muscles are very useful, but not just for fighting. As he runs on his epic missions, he can pick up and carry townspeople in need of rescue without even breaking a sweat!

Pneumatic drill

Businessman

This entrepreneur moved to Metroville because he wanted to meet the Incredibles.

57

MISSION Rooftop Rescue
MISSION GIVER Policeman

Three helpless citizens are trapped high on the rooftops of Metroville. They are very frightened and it's up to Mr Incredible to climb up the buildings and find them. It's all in a day's work for him!

1

To save this young boy, use strength and precision to throw him to safety within the yellow blockade circle.

MISSION Lock 'Em Up
MISSION GIVER Policeman

The local police force has asked Mr Incredible to help them round up all the crooks in Metroville. It's time that these lowdown rogues and hoodlums were all safely behind bars.

1

The criminals should be easy to spot – they're all wearing black-and-white striped clothes.

MISSION Bombs Galore
MISSION GIVER Rick Dicker

They don't call him Baron Von Ruthless for nothing. This no-good nobleman hid four bombs in Metroville. Mr Incredible must find them before they explode, turning the citizens into green monsters!

1

Use the compass to track down each bomb. The aim is to throw them into the fountain.

2 Climb to the next building and rescue the young girl the same way. There's no time to lose.

3 The final citizen is still on the first building. Climb to her rescue and toss her to safety, too.

100 COINS EARNED

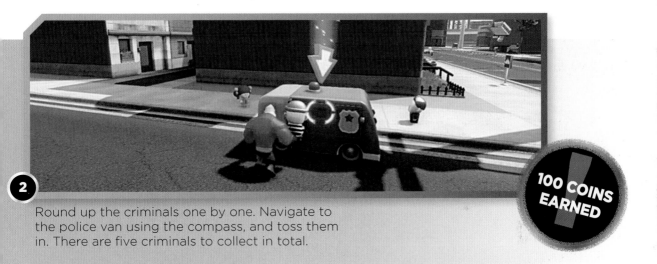

2 Round up the criminals one by one. Navigate to the police van using the compass, and toss them in. There are five criminals to collect in total.

100 COINS EARNED

2 Try to keep the citizens away from the bombs, but watch out for the Omnidroid foes, too.

3 Toss the bombs in the direction of the fountain. They can't do any harm if they're underwater.

500 COINS EARNED

MONSTERS UNIVERSITY

Welcome to Monsters University. Here you can study Science, Engineering, Business or Scaring, and learn all about the fine art of pranking. MU is a place to work hard – and play hard.

CONTENTS

SULLEY

James P. Sullivan, aka Sulley, was born to be a Scarer. Huge, horned and hairy, he has got the perfect monster look. Moreover, all his family are Scarers so it's in his DNA. Monsters University should be a breeze for a guy like him.

Pranking around
Sully would rather be playing pranks on Fear Tech students than hitting the books. He plans to toilet paper their whole campus!

PLAY TIP

Unlock the toilet paper launcher by completing the Remove the Rolls mission. **Buy it for 350 coins** and go on a pranking spree with Sulley.

Strange purple spots

Terrifying claws

GAME FILE

OCCUPATION: Scare student

SCARE PAL: Mike Wazowski

FAVOURITE PRANK: Anything involving the toilet paper launcher

FAVOURITE GADGETS

Toilet paper launcher   Bike

Giant, stompy feet

MIKE

Mike Wazowski has always dreamed of becoming a Scarer. He has studied hard and learned everything there is to know about Scaring. The trouble is it's hard to be scary when you're small, cute and green.

PLAY TIP

Unlock Fear Tech mascot Archie the Scare Pig by completing the Race to Victory mission. Then **use him in Mike's Scare Pig Dash challenge** for extra points.

GAME FILE

OCCUPATION: Scare student

SCARE PAL: James P. Sullivan

WOULD LOVE TO BE: A real Scarer

FAVOURITE GADGETS

Toilet paper launcher   Bike

One large eye

Cute horns

Scare tactics
This megaphone makes Mike sound like a fearsome beast when he needs a bit of help in the "being scary" department. It's great for waking up his pal, Sulley, too.

Perfect prankster
Mike might not be that scary but he is really good at playing pranks. When his pals kidnap Archie the Scare Pig, Mike hops on for a ride.

Skinny, green legs

Bony fingers

MU CAMPUS

ANOTHER DAY AT THE SCHOOL OF SCARING

Sulley climbs up this tall clock tower to rescue his friends, Terri and Terry, after Fear Tech students monster-nap them.

Beware of taking a flyer from this advertising column – a giant hand might shoot out and whack you!

This MU statue stands proudly on campus – but the Fear Tech students have covered it in toilet paper! Mike is on a mission to clear it up.

Who would dare to prank the MU campus?

RANDY

Randall Boggs wasn't always nasty. He used to be Mike Wazowski's roommate, but he decided that pranks and popularity were more important than friendship. Nowadays Randy is always looking for new ways to beat Mike and Sulley.

Spiky crest

GAME FILE
OCCUPATION: Scare student
PERSONALITY TYPE: Mean and sneaky
WOULD LOVE TO: Beat Sulley and Mike, be popular
FAVOURITE GADGETS

Prank boxing glove   Hand prank

PLAY TIP
Turn on Randy's sneak mode and **activate his cloaking ability**. This makes him invisible, which is perfect for one of his super sneaky missions.

Pearly white teeth

Long, swishy tail

Scaly skin changes colour

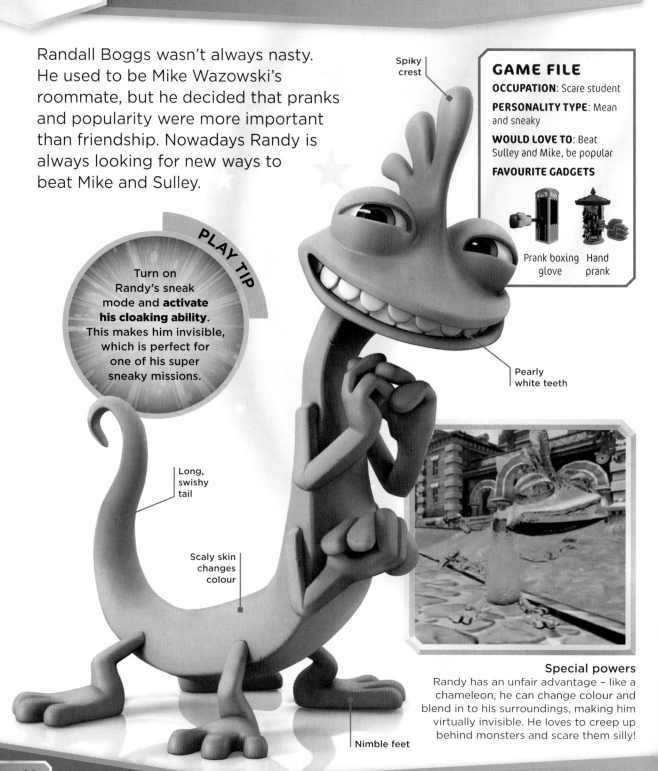

Special powers
Randy has an unfair advantage – like a chameleon, he can change colour and blend in to his surroundings, making him virtually invisible. He loves to creep up behind monsters and scare them silly!

Nimble feet

66

SQUISHY

Like his scare society buddy Mike, Scott "Squishy" Squibbles is not a natural Scarer. Shy, sweet and quiet, Squishy still lives with his mum. However, with the help of his Oozma Kappa fraternity pals, Squishy may find his inner monster.

Fear Tech invasion
Squishy isn't big or scary, but he is a great team player. Sulley may have the brawn to smash orange Fear Tech posters, but Squishy has the brains to find them in the first place.

GAME FILE

OCCUPATION: Student (subject undecided)

PERSONALITY TYPE: Gentle and kind

BIGGEST INFLUENCE: His mum

WOULD LIKE TO BE: Taller

One of five innocent eyes

Fraternity jumper

Small, cute hands

Oozma Kappa logo

Short, non-scary legs

PLAY TIP

Unlock the toilet paper launcher by completing Squishy's Roll Out mission. You will need it for the next mission – The Road to Fear Tech.

TOY BOX
ROOFTOP RUMBLE

Davy Jones' dastardly crew are tired of sailing the Seven Seas. They want to search for treasure at the MU campus! Mike is not about to let them ransack his school, so he calls in some backup to help him hold them off!

Zurgbots love a good battle. They're helping the pirates!

After the Kraken, Driftwood isn't scared of any monsters.

Yee-haw! Jessie is here with her frying pan to help Mike.

This pirate feels a bit wobbly climbing over a monster-shaped building.

PLAY TIP

It's a good idea to take part in the Combat Mastery Adventures in the Toy Box mode. It's a great way to **learn different techniques** to fight your enemies.

Maccus is just as scary on dry land as he is on the sea.

Mike has an unusual weapon – a flamingo croquet mallet.

Mrs Incredible is a skilled swordswoman. En garde!

FEAR TECH STUDENTS

The students of Monsters University believe that their college is the best in the world – the trouble is their neighbours, Fear Tech, think the same about their university! The rivalry between the two institutions is fierce and they love to play pranks on each other. These Fear Tech students are determined to prove that they are better than MU.

Sharp horn

Lucky shirt

Three eyes

Big brawny beast
This Fear Tech alumnus isn't the cleverest monster in school, but he is naturally tough and scary.

Hoops dude
This student loves playing pranks. His speciality is slam-dunking paint balloons on MU students.

Stick 'em up!

It is mayhem on campus as Fear Tech and MU students have a huge fight with their paintball shooters. Sulley is cornered by Fear Tech students and must put up his paws in surrender, as his opponents threaten to splat him!

PLAY TIP

Use the **Poloski sneak and scream technique** to scare the Fear Tech students. Just sneak up behind them and scream loudly when they least expect it.

Head-mounted torch

Scared eyes

Peaked cap

Patrol buddy
This big, green monster also patrols the Fear Tech campus. Fortunately for Sulley and friends, he is very bad at pranks.

Student patrol
This student patrols the campus at night, ready to thwart any of MU's midnight pranks.

Scared Scarer
This guy puts the "fear" into Fear Tech. He's a timid monster who'd rather be playing sports than pranks.

MISCHIEF AND DECORATION

UNLEASH THE TOILET PAPER AND GET PRANKING

MISSION Student Aid
MISSION GIVER Squishy

Squishy has heard that an MU student has been pranked by some Fear Tech monsters. The victim is terrified, trapped on the library roof and covered in toilet paper! Can Sulley rescue him?

1 Scare this one-eyed monster so he leaps out of the ground. Jump on a platform to get a boost up.

MISSION Statue Upgrade
MISSION GIVER Don Carlton

Don Carlton might be a mature student, but he's still up for a few pranks. Besides, it's time those Fear Tech creeps had a little payback, MU style. Get ready with the toilet paper launcher!

1 Sneak onto the Fear Tech campus and approach their statues. Don't let the guards see and chase you.

MISSION A Lesson in Pride
MISSION GIVER Blue Winged Monster

MU students are proud of their school and they want the world to know it. The blue winged monster has a bright idea – decorate the Fear Tech campus with four MU banners. Time to climb!

1 Climb on the roof of the Door Design School and slide along the yellow wire to unroll the first banner.

2

Shin up the drainpipe to the roof. Hold on tight though, as it's a long way down!

3

Locate the poor prank victim and scare it in order to break its toilet paper shackles. Freedom!

200 COINS EARNED

2

Get hit too many times and you end up in a locked room. Jump down on the vent and break through to escape.

3

Quickly fire the TP launcher to cover two statues, without getting caught.

250 COINS EARNED

2

Cross the wire on the library rooftop to release the next banner. Fear Tech never looked so good!

3

Finally, slide across the wires on the Botany building to unveil the last two banners. Job done!

250 COINS EARNED

Kooky Art is a one-in-a-million monster. The furry free spirit is a philosophy student, and it is rumoured that he has spent time in jail! Thanks to his passion for yoga, Art is surprisingly flexible and acrobatic. He is also a great dancer.

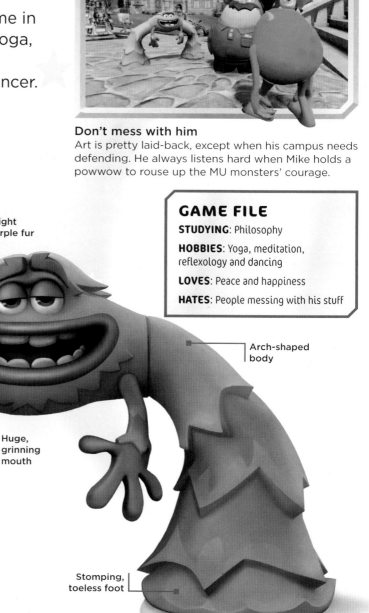

Don't mess with him
Art is pretty laid-back, except when his campus needs defending. He always listens hard when Mike holds a powwow to rouse up the MU monsters' courage.

PLAY TIP

Art's clock tower missions are not compulsory, but you will get extra credit: **completing these missions** will earn you 600 coins!

GAME FILE

STUDYING: Philosophy

HOBBIES: Yoga, meditation, reflexology and dancing

LOVES: Peace and happiness

HATES: People messing with his stuff

Bright purple fur

Arch-shaped body

Huge, grinning mouth

Four-fingered hands

Stomping, toeless foot

TERRI AND TERRY

Isn't it annoying when your sibling won't leave you alone? Twins Terri and Terry Perry couldn't agree more, but they're stuck with each other. They're inseparable, so wherever one goes, the other must go, too. It's a real bind – and do these two argue about it!

Terri has one horn

Terry is slightly taller

Terry has two horns

GAME FILE

TERRI LIKES: Looking on the bright side

DISLIKES: Being slightly shorter than his brother

TERRY LIKES: Thinking the worst

DISLIKES: Whatever his brother likes

Waving one of their four arms

PLAY TIP

Complete Terri and Terry's Nightmare Capers missions and **unlock the incoming call ender toy**. It's a handy gadget for pulling pranks.

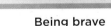

Being brave
Terri and Terry help their Oozma Kappa teammates by spying on Fear Tech rivals. However, they are captured and end up tied to the top of the MU clock tower. Sulley climbs up scaffolding, a ladder and a pipe to rescue them!

One of six stripy legs

ARCHIE

Monsters University's rival college, Fear Tech, is very proud of its mascot – Archie the Scare Pig. Archie is certainly no cute farmyard animal. This petrifying porker has bright orange fur, six legs, two horns and really scary eyes.

PLAY TIP

Unlock Archie by completing the Race to Victory mission in the Play Set. **Buy him for 1,500 coins** and then use him in the Toy Box.

GAME FILE

LIVES: In a pen on the Fear Tech campus

SECRET TALENT: Galloping really fast

SECRET DREAM: To be the MU mascot

Bulging eyes

Stabbing horns

Cosy blanket

Bright orange fur

Giddy up, pig
Sulley plans to free Archie and ends up riding him around the Fear Tech campus, causing plenty of mayhem. Archie is a pretty fast piggy when he wants to be.

DON CARLTON

Former salesmonster Don Carlton has decided to switch careers and become a Scarer. The mature student hopes he can be a positive role model for his fellow Monsters University alumni, and prove that you're never too old to follow your dreams.

Fraternity founder
Don Carlton helped set up the Oozma Kappa fraternity. He makes plans with Mike, Art and Terri and Terry to pull some jokes on the Fear Tech students, like covering them in sludge. Don might be a mature student, but he is just a big kid at heart!

Reading glasses

Tight-fitted t-shirt

Bushy moustache

Useful, but sometimes annoying suckers

GAME FILE

OCCUPATION:
Salesmonster-turned-Scarer

BEST FEATURE:
Suckers on his tentacles – they're great for climbing

WORST FEATURE:
Suckers on his tentacles – they're so noisy

PLAY TIP

Dodge security guards and **try to cover Fear Tech statues in toilet paper** in Don's Statue Upgrade mission. If the screen turns red, a guard has seen you.

TOY BOX
FUN AT THE BEACH

Even heroes deserve a holiday. Sulley and Mike are off to the beach and they've invited their pals Mr Incredible, Captain Jack Sparrow and Bullseye for some sun, sea and sand. Last one to the sea buys the ice creams!

Sulley is keen for a game of beach volleyball.

This Omnidroid should have stayed in the shade – his metal body is overheating!

Mr Incredible wants a gentle game of beach croquet.

The girls of MU sorority Python Nu Kappa have their home right on the beachfront!

Captain Jack and Bullseye can't wait for a dip in the ocean.

Mike doesn't feel very relaxed right now!

PLAY TIP

Gather as many collectibles as possible in three minutes in Mike's Scare Pig Adventure. Scoring 200 points will earn you a gold medal.

Monsters University prides itself on offering a range of different courses to its diverse students. There is something to suit everyone here, from shy, bookish monsters to big sporty ones. While some students, such as Sulley and Mike, love being the centre of attention, others just like to stay under the radar.

GAME FILE:

MOST LIKELY TO GET HOMESICK:
Red winged monster

MOST LIKELY TO INVENT A NEW HAIRSTYLE: Blue striped monster

MOST LIKELY TO HIT A HOME RUN:
Yellow monster

MOST LIKELY TO HIDE UNDER HIS BED:
Light blue monster

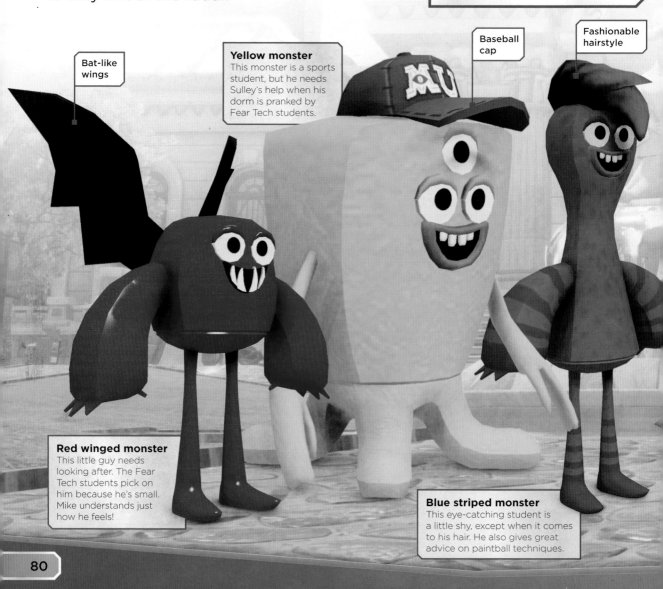

Bat-like wings

Baseball cap

Fashionable hairstyle

Yellow monster
This monster is a sports student, but he needs Sulley's help when his dorm is pranked by Fear Tech students.

Red winged monster
This little guy needs looking after. The Fear Tech students pick on him because he's small. Mike understands just how he feels!

Blue striped monster
This eye-catching student is a little shy, except when it comes to his hair. He also gives great advice on paintball techniques.

PLAY TIP

These funny-looking monsters are actually quite important. **Take part in their missions** in the MU Play Set and collect major points.

Helping hand

The purple monster might be forgetful but she has plenty of school spirit. When Sulley sneaks up on a Fear Tech student who has been trespassing, she keeps a lookout. No one messes with her campus!

Extra-sharp horns

Extra-long eyelashes

Long tentacles

Library book

Short arms

Light blue monster
This monster isn't brave enough to help his pals when Fear Tech students make them wear their logo, but his friend Sulley is.

Purple monster
This forgetful student is always losing things. She had a bunch of Fear-It Week tokens, but they fell out of a hole in her backpack!

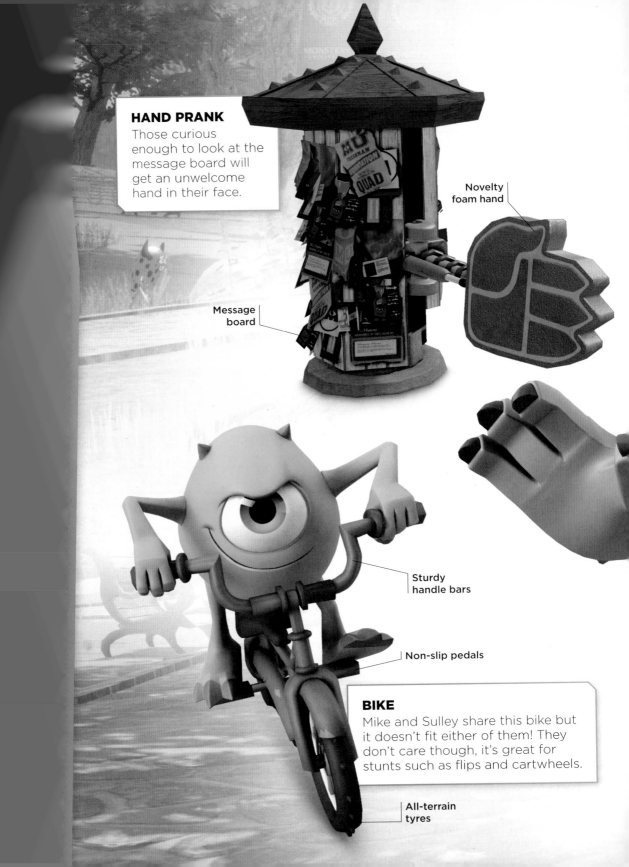

HAND PRANK
Those curious enough to look at the message board will get an unwelcome hand in their face.

Novelty foam hand

Message board

Sturdy handle bars

Non-slip pedals

BIKE
Mike and Sulley share this bike but it doesn't fit either of them! They don't care though, it's great for stunts such as flips and cartwheels.

All-terrain tyres

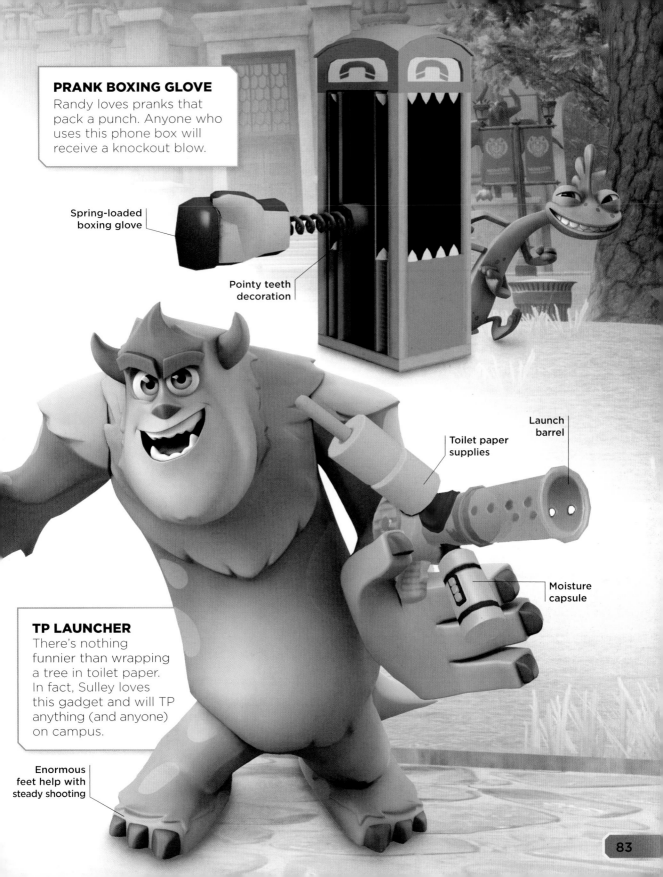

PRANK BOXING GLOVE
Randy loves pranks that pack a punch. Anyone who uses this phone box will receive a knockout blow.

Spring-loaded boxing glove

Pointy teeth decoration

Toilet paper supplies

Launch barrel

Moisture capsule

TP LAUNCHER
There's nothing funnier than wrapping a tree in toilet paper. In fact, Sulley loves this gadget and will TP anything (and anyone) on campus.

Enormous feet help with steady shooting

CARS

Take a drive down to Radiator Springs. It's a quirky but friendly little town in the middle of the desert. The residents are very welcoming, just as long as you like to race!

CONTENTS

LIGHTNING MCQUEEN

Lightning is the fastest thing on four wheels, and also one of the nicest. He loves to race and he also loves helping his friends. Lightning certainly has a lot of pals in Radiator Springs.

PLAY TIP

When Lightning McQueen needs more missions, use Finn McMissile for challenging tasks. To activate Finn **purchase Sarge's Surplus Hut**.

Off road
Lightning loves a challenge, from flying over ramps in the desert to helping his friend Mater out of his latest scrape. He'll try anything – as long as it involves speed.

Rear spoiler with flame design

State-of-the-art headlights

MATER

Lovable fool Mater can hardly remember what his life was like before Lightning McQueen came to Radiator Springs. Since his best pal's arrival, Mater has been on one thrilling adventure after another. Mater has never been happier!

Special talent
Mater's job is to find broken-down cars and tow them to safety. He also has a secret talent – he's an expert at driving backwards.

Rusty roof

PLAY TIP
Take part in Mater's Tow 'n' Go Adventure and **haul as many cars as possible** to their destination. Every car towed earns spins to open the Toy Box Vault.

Missing headlight

Tow hook

GAME FILE

OCCUPATION: Tow truck

BEST FRIEND: Lightning McQueen

HOBBIES: Tractor tipping

MOST LIKELY TO: Have an accidental adventure

FAVOURITE GADGET

Monster truck tyres

RADIATOR SPRINGS
A FRIENDLY DESERT TOWN

The Cozy Cone Motel is the perfect rest spot for weary travellers. Any car is welcome, from race cars to station wagons or touring vehicles.

Radiator Springs is a quiet, peaceful town. The courthouse hasn't been used since Lightning McQueen first arrived.

Some people say that Flo's V8 Café is the best restaurant in the state. If you don't believe them, drive in and try it for yourself!

Welcome to Radiator Springs. Drive safely!

Many different cars like to call Radiator Springs "home", but these three are probably the most unusual. They have all travelled the world and had many amazing adventures, but they agree that nowhere beats Radiator Springs. There is just something special about this dusty old town.

PLAY TIP

Pop three red balloons placed by Guido at the Stunt Park in the Balloon Poppin' mission. This simple mission can earn you 500 coins.

Groovy flower design

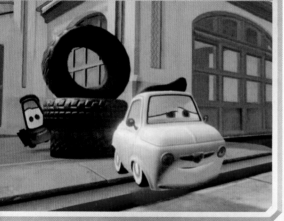

Friendly pranks
Guido loves playing tricks on his friend Luigi. His favourite prank is to hide so his pal has to go looking for him. Unfortunately, Guido is so small that Luigi can never find him!

Special blades for lifting and screwing

Guido
This tiny forklift truck has two huge passions in life: fast cars and tyres.

Expert advice
Easy-going Fillmore likes to take his time and just enjoy a gentle ride. Speedy Lightning, on the other hand, takes great pleasure in zooming down the road.

PLAY TIP

Use multiple tow cables to **drag five tractors** in Fillmore's Tractor Rescue mission. The cables are strong enough to haul lots of tractors in one go.

Roof folds back

Fillmore
Laid-back Fillmore cares a lot about the environment and likes to stay in touch with nature.

Luigi
This excitable Italian loves racing and running his own shop, Casa della Tires, in Radiator Springs.

HOLLEY SHIFTWELL

Rookie spy Holley Shiftwell works for the British Secret Service. She has read all the manuals and is equipped with all the latest gadgets. She can't wait to put her training into action. Sleek, smart and speedy, Holley is ready for any mission.

GAME FILE

OCCUPATION: Spy (trainee)

SPECIAL ABILITIES: Tight manoeuvres, undercover work

FAVOURITE BOOK: Spy manual

FAVOURITE GADGETS

Machine gun   Towable ramp

Sharp shooter
Holley is armed with a state-of-the-art machine gun. With a burst of rapid fire she can quickly disarm her enemies, without scratching her own perfect paintwork.

PLAY TIP

Grind on special rails and pick up gas tanks to gain turbo in a race. This will boost Holley's speed in case she falls behind her competitors.

Sleek, purple exterior

Moveable wing mirrors

Compact rear

FRANCESCO

Some might call Italian race car Francesco Bernoulli arrogant, but he prefers "confident". He has won many races and has fans across the globe, so it's no surprise that he's a bit of a show-off. Deep down though, Francesco is a good guy.

GAME FILE

NATIONALITY: Italian

OCCUPATION: Race car

PERSONALITY TYPE: Super-confident

RACING TIP: To be the best you must practise racing every day.

FAVOURITE GADGETS

Machine gun   Missile

Friendly rivals
Francesco believes that he is faster than Lightning McQueen and is keen to prove it. Although he has yet to actually beat his rival, Francesco won't give up trying!

Loudspeaker

Race number

PLAY TIP

Do not skip optional challenges such as Tow the Speeder or Rescue the Tourist. It's a quick way for Francesco to earn extra coins.

Racing tyres

TOY BOX
SHOWING OFF

Lightning McQueen used to be a real show-off and sometimes he still can't resist dazzling his pals with a daring stunt. He has been practising this one for weeks. It involves powering up a steep ramp and then executing a perfect backflip.

Jack Skellington is raring to have a go on the ramp, too.

Mr Incredible thinks he might try a stunt next!

These safety barriers will protect Lightning if anything goes wrong.

PLAY TIP

Completing the Driving Mastery Adventure will earn you a Mastery Star and a Spin. You will also unlock other Adventures, such as Battle Race and Lap Race.

Lightning used this ramp to practise his stunt.

Syndrome is jealous of Lightning's natural talent.

Buzz is super impressed and can't wait to tell Woody.

The ramp is pretty high, but Lightning's Monster Truck Tires keep him churning along with their mighty grip and power.

MISSION Cave Race
MISSION GIVER Yellow Race Car

A sporty little yellow car wants to test his speed against legendary Lightning McQueen on a treacherous cave track. The caves are cleared of debris, but it will take skill to manoeuvre the many twists and turns.

1 Get ready, set, go! The race lasts for two laps, so pump the accelerator to get a fast start.

MISSION Jump into the Barn
MISSION GIVER Little Grey Car

One little car doesn't think it is possible to jump through the barn. He has obviously never met Lightning McQueen before! And if there's one thing that Lightning can't resist, it's a challenge...

1 Press the button on the silo to position the ramp ready in front of the barn.

MISSION Chick's Challenge
MISSION GIVER Chick Hicks

Chick Hicks is desperate to beat Lightning McQueen so he has challenged him to a race. It will be three laps, and Chick is planning to go out hard right from the start. Let the battle begin!

1 It's crucial to match Chick for speed and power. Rev the engine and max out the turbo meter for a fast start.

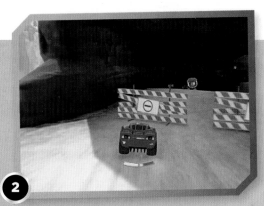

2

Take a shortcut through the caves to get ahead. Will the yellow car be brave enough to follow?

3

Secure victory by drifting into the turns and hit the turbo for a boost of speed on straight patches.

TURBO LEVEL 1 UNLOCKED

2

Deploy the turbo so that there is enough speed when you hit the ramp. Reach the top section of the barn, then drive out the rest of the way and sail to victory!

100 COINS EARNED

2

Take shortcuts to skip some track, like jumping off the springing platform at Sarge's Surplus Hut. Don't worry if Chick sneaks ahead – overtake with a turbo boost.

250 COINS EARNED

CHICK HICKS

Chick Hicks wants to win, and he doesn't care how he does it. The veteran racer has been round the track more than a few times and hates being a runner-up. Chick will use any dirty trick he can think of to grab first place.

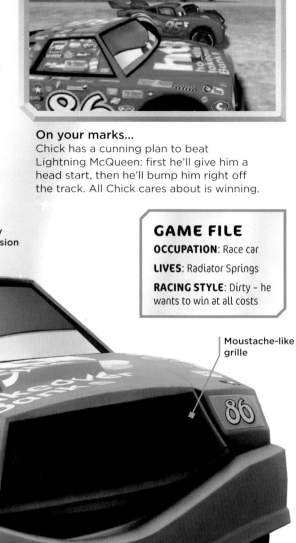

PLAY TIP

In the Chick's Challenge mission, play the wily race car at his own game – **use the springing platform** in front of Sarge's Surplus Hut to leap ahead in the race.

On your marks...

Chick has a cunning plan to beat Lightning McQueen: first he'll give him a head start, then he'll bump him right off the track. All Chick cares about is winning.

Sneaky expression

GAME FILE

OCCUPATION: Race car

LIVES: Radiator Springs

RACING STYLE: Dirty – he wants to win at all costs

Sponsors' logos stuck all over chassis

Moustache-like grille

RAMONE

Ramone doesn't simply repair scratched or damaged paintwork, he makes it look better than it did before. He is full of amazing ideas and he loves sharing them with his friends and customers at Ramone's House of Body Art. People travel from miles around for a makeover from Ramone.

Secret ambitions

Ramone would love to share his talents with the world and dreams of taking part in a TV show called *Detail My Dents*. His pal Luigi understands perfectly – he secretly longs to be a sleek, turbo-charged Ferrari. Keep dreaming, boys!

PLAY TIP

Help to restore Radiator Springs after a terrible storm in Ramone's Storm Damage mission. Earn 300 coins when **you repair the buildings**.

Sleek body

Eyelids to protect against the sun's glare when racing

GAME FILE

OCCUPATION: Artist

STYLE: Street art with a fantasy twist

MARRIED TO: Flo

Trademark body art flames

Personalised detail

Stylish yellow hubcaps

TOY BOX
VANELLOPE'S VICTORY

Unusually, Lightning McQueen and Francesco Bernoulli are competing for second place in this race – because Vanellope von Schweetz has first place in the bag! Syndrome is breaking the rules, as usual, so he will definitely be disqualified.

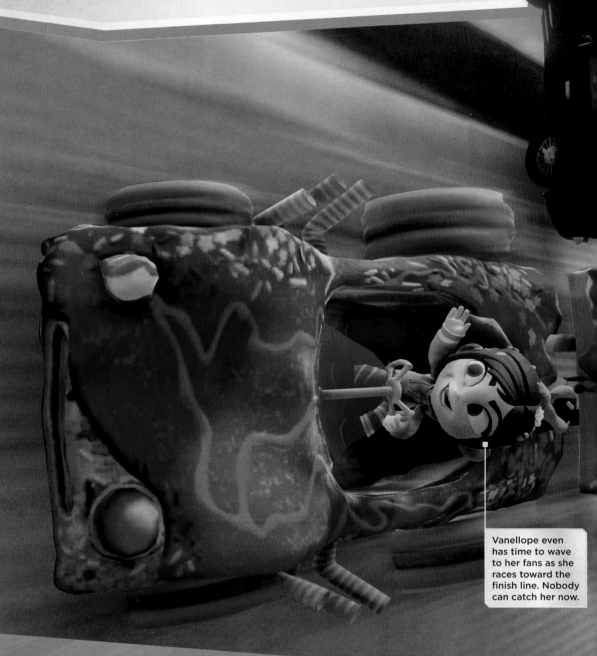

Vanellope even has time to wave to her fans as she races toward the finish line. Nobody can catch her now.

Syndrome is not only breaking the rules, he is doing it in Mr Incredible's car!

PLAY TIP

To grab a high score in Francesco's Rush Adventure, **use shortcuts**. You can find a secret one as you approach the first left turn – drive straight forward instead of turning.

Francesco appears to have taken the last corner a little too sharply. He is in danger of flipping over.

This safety barrier ensures that the cars will be safe if they crash.

Lightning doesn't enjoy losing, but he knows that Vanellope deserves the victory. He will beat her next time though!

FLO

As the owner of Flo's V8 Café in Radiator Springs, Flo provides refreshing fuel and a sympathetic ear to anyone lucky enough to be passing through the town. Cars from far and wide drop in for a sip of oil with a side order of Flo's great advice.

PLAY TIP

Help Flo save Radiator Springs in the Bales of Fire mission. **Put out the fire** before the whole town goes up in smoke!

It's business
Flo wants the V8 Café to be the hottest hangout in the county, so she always tries to think of new ways to create publicity. Mater's daring jump across the ramps will surely put the café on the map!

GAME FILE
OCCUPATION: Café owner
MARRIED TO: Ramone
BEST ADVICE: Always be yourself

Past glories
A vintage 1950s show car, Flo is one of a kind. She used to be a famous dancer, but now she prefers to live a quieter life in good old Radiator Springs.

Stylish aqua paintwork

Retro spoilers

Sleek bonnet

FINN

Charming, intelligent and brave, Finn McMissile is the perfect spy. He is ready for anything – undercover work, quick getaways, high-speed shoot-outs – and usually emerges without a scratch on his perfect paintwork. Best of all, Finn is also a really nice guy.

I spy
Finn rarely takes a break from his job. Even when he is supposed to be on holiday in Radiator Springs, he gives the locals some spy training!

PLAY TIP

Try the Finn's Wrong Turn mission and help him **find five tourist cars that have gone missing** after a storm hits Radiator Springs. Win 500 coins if you succeed.

Reinforced bulletproof body

Missile launcher (in headlight)

GAME FILE

NATIONALITY: British

LIKES: That's classified information

DISLIKES: Bad guys

MISSION Corny Concoction
MISSION GIVER Fillmore

Fillmore is always looking for new fuel ideas. There's only one rule – they must be 100 percent organic. Fillmore is working on a special recipe, but he needs help sourcing ingredients.

1 Follow the compass to find corn for Fillmore and collect it with the tow cable.

MISSION Race the King
MISSION GIVER Dark Gray Car

Luigi has built a fantastic new track in Radiator Springs. It looks superb, but how does it drive? The King has challenged Lightning McQueen to a test race. Engines ready? Let's race!

1 This is a complex, winding track. It's going to take precision as well as speed to get round it.

MISSION Double Back Dash
MISSION GIVER Luigi

Lightning McQueen is about to face one of his toughest tests yet: a new reverse track. Japanese race car Shu Todoroki has challenged him to a race – may the best car win!

1 This is an unusual course so it is a wise idea to get familiar with it by navigating some practice circuits.

2

Once the corn is attached, tow it back to Fillmore's place and drop it off at the mixer near the giant, colourful barrels.

50 SPARKS EARNED

2

There are lots of detours and alternative routes, but following the track is usually the quickest option.

3

If there is an alternative route with extra fuel cans, it may be a good choice. Power is key.

300 COINS EARNED

2

Look out for shortcuts on the course and use the drift manoeuvre to take the corners.

3

Save the turbo boost for the last lap and then use all your tactics to pass the chequered sign first.

500 COINS EARNED

Chain attaches
to rear bumper

Strong metal
chain

Tow
hook

Deep treads for
extra staying power

Extra
wide tyres

MONSTER TYRES
Mater's adventures can take him
through some rough terrain, but
he can handle anything with his
new monster tyres.

MISSILE
Francesco is not only fast – he
is fully loaded, too. At the push
of a button, a missile blast can
burst a tyre, blow up a building,
or distract an opponent.

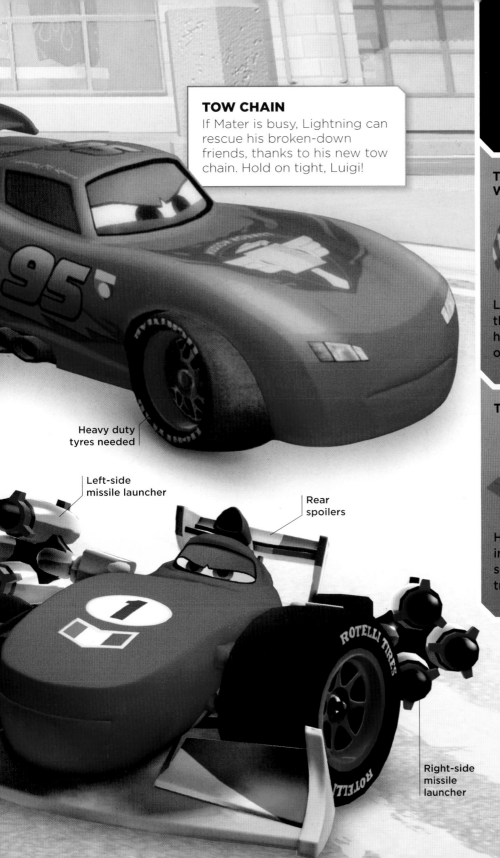

TOW CHAIN

If Mater is busy, Lightning can rescue his broken-down friends, thanks to his new tow chain. Hold on tight, Luigi!

Heavy duty tyres needed

Left-side missile launcher

Rear spoilers

Right-side missile launcher

TOWABLE WRECKING BALL

Faded yellow chevrons

Lightning can also attach this iron wrecking ball to his tow chain, to knock over any obstructions!

TOWABLE RAMP

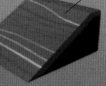

Steep gradient

Holley carries this, in case she needs some help with a tricky manoeuvre.

THE LONE RANGER

The Wild West is a dangerous and lawless place.
Villainous bandits roam the area, looking for stuff to steal,
shoot or blow up. Fortunately, one brave man, the Lone Ranger,
is willing to fight for justice – but he could use a little help.

CONTENTS

THE LONE RANGER

John Reid believes in justice, but sometimes he has to take the law into his own hands. As the Lone Ranger, masked hero Reid is prepared to fight to keep the Wild West safe.

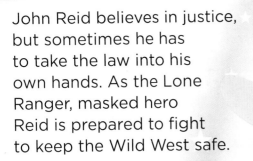

Pure white cowboy hat

Mask to hide identity

Badge of law

GAME FILE

ALIAS: John Reid

ALLY: Tonto

BELIEVES: That justice is worth fighting for

FAVOURITE GADGETS

Jupiter train   TNT pack

Shoot-out
When the Cavendish Gang attacks the town of Colby, the Lone Ranger doesn't hesitate to act. The sharp shooter shows the bandits that they messed with the wrong guy.

PLAY TIP
When you unlock the explosives pack in the Play Set, it allows the Lone Ranger to **toss dynamite** at his enemies. Watch out, Butch Cavendish!

Bang to rights
When the odds are stacked against him the Lone Ranger knows just what to do – blow the bandits sky high with some explosive TNT.

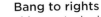

TONTO

Comanche Indian warrior Tonto is a spiritual man, who prefers animals and nature to people. He wants everyone to live in peace. However, like his friend John Reid, he knows that he may have to fight to achieve it.

Crow headdress

Painted face markings

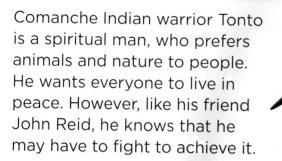

Brave allies
Tonto is proud to fight alongside the Lone Ranger. Together the two heroes are determined to bring peace and justice to the Wild West.

Protective breastplate

Animal friends
Tonto's love of animals often comes in useful. A friendly elephant makes a great battle steed – strong, loyal and rather intimidating for enemies!

GAME FILE
ALLY: Lone Ranger

LIKES: Nature, animals, peace

DISLIKES: Injustice, bullies

FAVOURITE GADGETS

Stagecoach

Elephant

PLAY TIP

Look out for the five bone charm locations dispersed throughout the Lone Ranger Play Set and **unlock Tonto's ability to fly**.

Horses are the easiest way to travel in the Wild West. Tired and hungry horses will be well cared for at Samuel's Livery Stable.

SAMUEL'S LIVERY STABLE.

LIVERY STABLE.

It's time the Lone Ranger brought justice to this town!

Times are tough in the Wild West, so business people deal in more than one trade. J.R. Stein specialises in both furniture and funerals.

Most people keep all their money in the town bank. So far, no one has ever tried to rob it, but Butch Cavendish's gang is lurking nearby...

TOY BOX
SYNDROME STRIKES

The Lone Ranger may have beaten the Cavendish Gang, but there's a new bad guy in town – Syndrome! The evil villain has stolen a glow urchin weapon from MU and is clearly up to mischief. But don't worry, the Lone Ranger has called in backup.

Woody feels right at home in the Wild West.

Tonto is always willing to help his pal.

The Lone Ranger will do anything to protect his town.

The glow urchin's stinging spikes make Syndrome's targets swell up painfully on contact.

Silver is the fastest horse in Colby.

TOY BOX

Target Butch's gang on horseback to get more points in the Lone Ranger's Justice Run Adventure. Each defeated rider earns you 10 points, but you only get 2 for crooks on foot.

Syndrome just loves to cause trouble!

Syndrome has stolen this getaway train.

BUTCH CAVENDISH

Butch Cavendish is a thoroughly bad man. He'll break any law in the land if he feels like it, and he'll pick a fight with anyone who gets in his way. He has assembled a gang of the worst outlaws in Texas to help him take over the town of Colby.

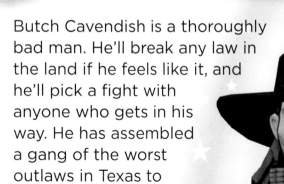

Sinister black hat

Straggly hair

Long, black coat

PLAY TIP

Follow instructions closely in the Nowhere to Hide mission. To beat Cavendish and his men, you must **destroy their hideout**, not the outlaws.

GAME FILE

OCCUPATION: Outlaw

LIKES: Stealing, blowing things up, generally breaking the law

DISLIKES: Being caught

SECRET FACT: Butch's real name is Bartholomew

Clever criminal
Butch is clever. His cunning plan is to rob every train on the railroad with his gang. If the Lone Ranger and Tonto try to stop them, they won't go down without a fight.

Black cowboy boots

It's personal
Butch keeps his mob close as they swagger down the street in an attack. It is a wise plan – the Lone Ranger wants revenge on Butch for killing his brother!

RED HARRINGTON

Merchant, saloon owner and promoter of lavish entertainments, Red is a woman of many talents. She is also the kind of person who knows a lot of useful information. However, she doesn't like to reveal too much about herself. Red even keeps her real first name a closely guarded secret.

Stylish hat perched on head

Mutual enemy
Red wants some cattle, so the Lone Ranger does her favour and delivers a herd over to Red's by train. In return, Red gives him TNT – she will do anything she can to help him beat her old enemy, Butch Cavendish.

Trademark red coat

Pretty dress

PLAY TIP

You need to **be quick on your feet** for Harrington's Chasin' Elephants mission. You only have 3 minutes and 20 seconds to finish the Cavendish Gang off.

GAME FILE

PERSONALITY TYPE: Calm, yet mysterious

FAVOURITE COLOUR: Red, of course

MOST LIKELY TO: Find that thing you really need

LEAST LIKELY TO: Tell you a secret

COWBOY OUTLAWS

Butch Cavendish plans to take control of the town of Colby and the nearby railroad. It's a big job and the townsfolk aren't going to like it. However, Butch has enlisted the help of the meanest, greediest, dirtiest bandits he can find. Together, these low-life lawbreakers will put the "wild" into Wild West.

GAME FILE
NOTABLE FEATURES: Thick beards and sideburns to hide their true identities

CRIMES: Building blockades on train tracks, blowing up jails, stealing TNT

FAMOUS THEFT: Pilfering an elephant from the Ringmaster of Red's entertainments

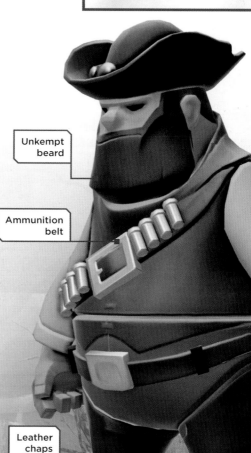

Armed and dangerous
These wicked outlaws shoot first and ask questions later. They show no mercy or compassion – they'll just ride in and blast anyone who gets in their way. Fortunately, the Lone Ranger doesn't like bullies – and he's a sharp shooter, too.

Unkempt beard

Ammunition belt

Leather chaps

Shotgun man
This outlaw always carries plenty of spare bullets for his shotgun. He can hit his target from an impressive distance.

PLAY TIP

The Cavendish Gang are a menace. **Try to shoot them down** in various missions and earn yourself some handy points.

Cowboy hat, worn low

Boss man
As long as Butch Cavendish pays them, this heartless band of outlaws will do whatever he tells them to. They don't care about the law or people's property.

Trusty sticks of dynamite

Fringed jacket

Pistol man
This bandit's weapon of choice is the pistol. It is great for firing at enemies from close range.

TNT man
Boom! This ruffian's job is to blow up railroads, or whole towns. It is risky work, but he loves a good explosion.

MISSION Clearin' the Rails
MISSION GIVER Train Engineer

The Cavendish Gang has a fiendish plan to sabotage the railroad. They've built blockades so the trains can't run. Someone must stop them before there is an accident.

1 The first blockade is near the water tower. Destroy it with a few sticks of TNT. Watch out for outlaws!

MISSION Aimin' High
MISSION GIVER Lady Sharpshooter

The mysterious Lady Sharpshooter has set the Lone Ranger a challenge. If he thinks he's the best shot in the Wild West, he had better step up and prove it!

1 First, use your climbing skills to get to the top of these rocky mountains.

MISSION Chasin' Elephants
MISSION GIVER Red Harrington

Who says the Cavendish Gang doesn't have a sense of humour? The outlaws have stolen an elephant! Red isn't laughing though, as they've stolen some of her money, too.

1 Set off in hot pursuit and track down the first bandit by following the red arrows.

2

Follow the tracks to the station, and find the second blockade on the right. Blow it sky high!

3

The third and final blockade is to the left of the station. Take out the rest of the outlaws, too.

250 COINS EARNED

2

Next, jump onto a narrow yellow ledge, run to the right, and find a short tunnel. Don't look down!

3

Finally, climb up the wooden planks and hit the target with a single shot.

100 COINS EARNED

2

Locate the rest of the bandits near the lumber station and take them out. Then hop on the elephant and ride him back to safety.

250 COINS EARNED

SHERIFF

The Sheriff of Colby is a fine, upstanding man. He prides himself on keeping the law-abiding citizens of his little town safe. However, thanks to the Cavendish Gang, the Sheriff has a big problem on his hands. He is going to need some serious backup.

Sheriff's hat

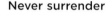

Never surrender
The Sheriff is darn sure that Butch Cavendish needs to be taught a lesson. He may need the Lone Ranger's help to save Colby, but he has a few ideas of his own, too.

Old friends
The Sheriff's friend the Train Engineer agrees that there is only one person who can help them save Colby – the Lone Ranger.

Shiny sheriff's badge

Sleeves rolled up for action

PLAY TIP

Follow the Sheriff's lead in the Ranch Hand mission. **Chase the Cavendish Gang away from the ranch** and earn 500 points after you are done.

GAME FILE

ALLIES: The Lone Ranger, Tonto

ENEMIES: Butch Cavendish and his gang

LIKES: A nice, quiet town

DISLIKES: Lawbreakers

Sturdy boots for patrolling the town

TRAIN ENGINEER

Trains may be the quickest way to travel across the Wild West, but they are not always the safest. Outlaws often lie in wait to rob the passengers or steal the cargo. Driving a train is a dangerous job, but the tough Train Engineer loves it.

Peaked cap

PLAY TIP

Help the Train Engineer **remove blockades from the train tracks** in the Clearin' The Rails mission. You'll earn 250 coins once the tracks are clear.

GAME FILE

OCCUPATION: Train engineer

PERSONALITY: Brave, determined, hardworking

LIKES: Making sure that the trains run on time

DISLIKES: People interfering with the railroad

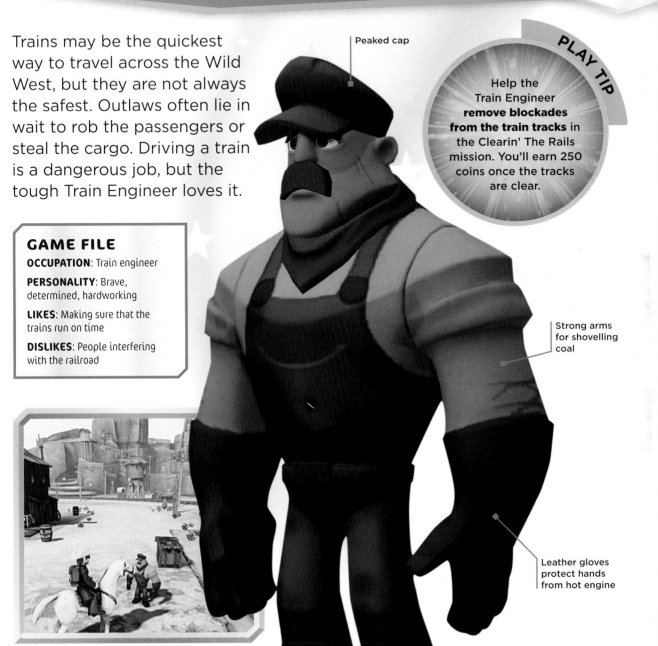

Strong arms for shovelling coal

Leather gloves protect hands from hot engine

Grime-covered trousers

Trouble on the tracks
The Engineer has a big problem – the Cavendish Gang has completely blockaded the railroad. He needs the Lone Ranger's help to clear the tracks and get the trains running again.

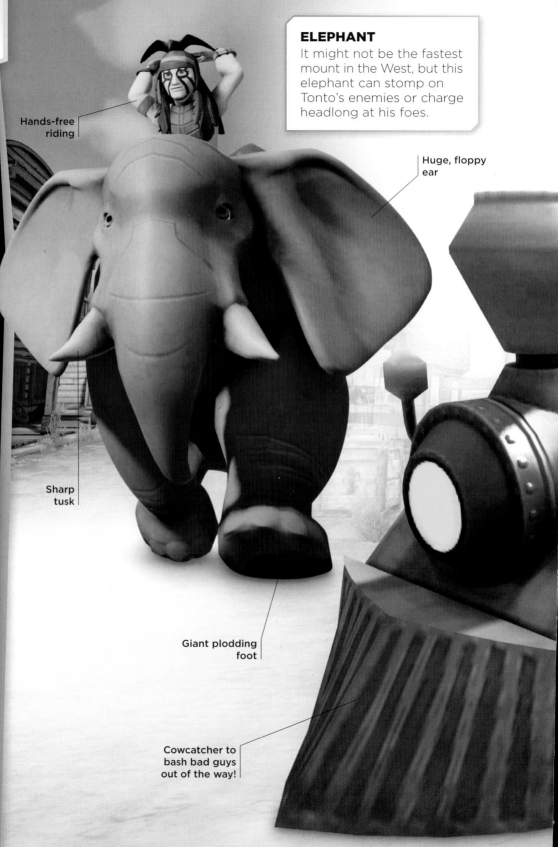

Hands-free riding

ELEPHANT
It might not be the fastest mount in the West, but this elephant can stomp on Tonto's enemies or charge headlong at his foes.

Huge, floppy ear

Sharp tusk

Giant plodding foot

Cowcatcher to bash bad guys out of the way!

Smokestack with spark catcher

Steering wheel (unusual for a train)

Padded carriage

STAGECOACH

Wooden crates

Rickety wheels

This classic Wild West vehicle is perfect for moving goods and is surprisingly fast.

TNT PACK

Red stick of dynamite

This pack of explosives can blow blockades or bandits sky high.

Rumbling wheels race along

Piston drives wheels

JUPITER TRAIN

Sometimes, the Lone Ranger prefers steam power to horse power, so he gives Silver a rest and rides this mechanical marvel instead. The *Jupiter* is great for patrolling the desert.

TOY BOX
ON YOUR MARKS...

Mrs Incredible thought it would be fun to organise a crazy derby with some of her pals! She is riding mighty Phillipe, but the Lone Ranger has swapped Silver for a strange alien horse, Maximus is carrying Mike and Tonto is on his trusty elephant.

Tonto is just happy to spend time with his elephant friend. Winning doesn't matter to him.

The elephant only hopes that he doesn't finish in last place.

PLAY TIP

When Tonto isn't riding elephants, he is soaring over the desert with his crow wings. **Make sure you explore the caves** in Tonto's Flight Adventure.

TOY STORY

Life is no longer a game for these brave toys – their adventures just got real. They need to step up and show the galaxy what they are made of. To infinity and beyond!

CONTENTS

WOODY

Other toys look up to Sheriff Woody and follow his lead. Dependable and decisive, he always seems to know what to do for the best. Woody was made for Wild West adventures, but he'll go anywhere he's needed.

Dashing cowboy hat

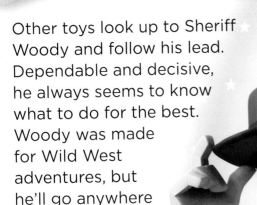

Giddy up, partner!
Woody always relies on his brave toy horse, Bullseye, to carry him into the middle of an adventure and to be there when he needs to make a quick getaway.

GAME FILE

OCCUPATION: Sheriff

PERSONALITY TYPE: Calm and courageous

GREATEST QUALITY: Leadership

WORST QUALITY: Being suspicious

FAVOURITE GADGET

Bullseye

Star-shaped sheriff's badge

Bright checked shirt

Cowboy to the rescue
Woody helps the aliens and new species on an action-packed planet. He finds the eggs and bring them to the hatchery. This pink Boomeroid critter used to be one of the eggs!

PLAY TIP

You need to be quick on your feet in Woody's Round-Up Adventure. To win a gold medal you must **complete the three-lap race** in under three minutes.

Toy spurs

BUZZ LIGHTYEAR

Buzz Lightyear has sworn to protect the galaxy and he takes his job very seriously. Life as a space ranger can be exciting, but also very dangerous. However, Buzz is not scared to get stuck in and help the aliens on their new planet – in fact, he is raring to go!

Protective hood keeps in heat on cold planets

GAME FILE

OCCUPATION: Space ranger

PERSONALITY TYPE: Focused, brave and a tiny bit shy

FUN FACT: Deep down, Buzz is a real romantic.

SECRET CRUSH: Jessie

FAVOURITE GADGETS

Jetpack

Star command blaster

Space ranger logo

Strong shoulder armour for charging into enemies

Wrist communicator

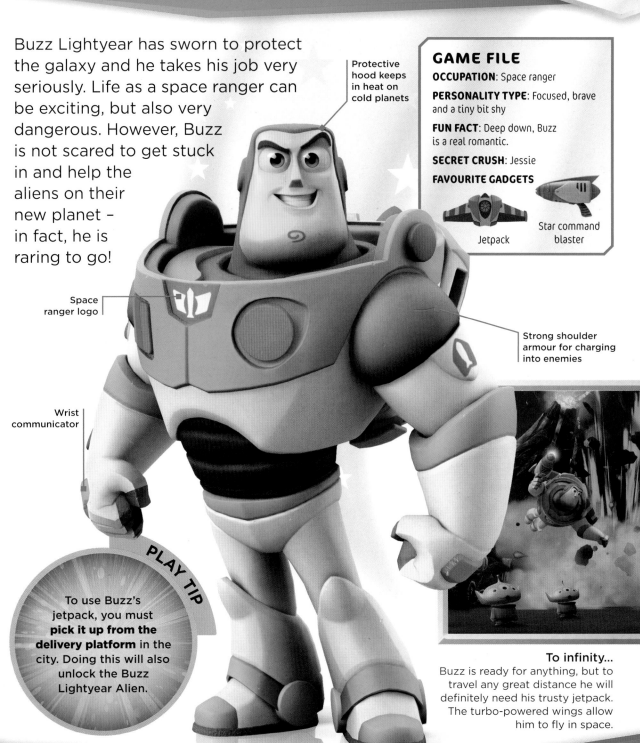

PLAY TIP

To use Buzz's jetpack, you must **pick it up from the delivery platform** in the city. Doing this will also unlock the Buzz Lightyear Alien.

To infinity...
Buzz is ready for anything, but to travel any great distance he will definitely need his trusty jetpack. The turbo-powered wings allow him to fly in space.

MISSION Power the Tower
MISSION GIVER Rex

The alien planet is being pelted with volcanic debris, but the Shield Generator isn't working. Buzz and the gang must restore the power and raise the Shield.

1 Use the compass to locate the green and yellow Shield Generator tower. Head toward it, quick as you can.

MISSION The Crystal Cavern
MISSION GIVER Hamm

Hamm has heard a rumour that one of the aliens has found a cave full of powerful crystals. This could be big news, but the gang had better find that cave before Zurg does.

1 Use the compass to locate two ledges at the rear of the Shield Generator tower.

MISSION Alien Liberation
MISSION GIVER Alien

One of the little green guys has got lost. He is behind a huge wall, and he can't get out. He is scared and very lonely. Somebody needs to help him! Buzz Lightyear to the rescue!

1 If you have a jetpack, use it to zoom straight up and over the high wall.

2

Summon every bit of strength to lift the huge power batteries and slot them into the right spot.

3

Take the lift to the top of the tower and look for a big button marked "IN". Push it!

25 CRYSTALS EARNED

2

Leap onto the ledges until you find a waterfall. The cave is above it, to the right.

3

Enter the cave and find the crystals. Smash the crystals, especially the golden ones.

50 CRYSTALS EARNED

2

If not, take a dip in the purple pool, in order to shrink down small. Squeeze through a hole in the wall.

3

Find the alien on the other side. Pick him up and jump over the platforms to bring him to safety.

50 CRYSTALS EARNED

JESSIE

Fearless, fun and full of energy, Jessie is just the kind of toy you want in your gang. She's tough and brave and will do anything to help her friends. Jessie loves the thrill of a new adventure – it's so satisfying to beat a bad guy. Yee-haw!

Wide-brimmed cowgirl hat

Dirty work
Jessie throws herself into every adventure with gusto, no matter how dangerous. She teams up with Buzz Lightyear to launch a fierce goo attack on Zurg and his space villains.

Red yarn plaits

Fancy cuffs

PLAY TIP

Jessie's ability to communicate with critters can be very handy. Use it to **seek help in tricky situations** and move ahead in the game.

Synthetic cowhide chaps

Goo lose!
Jessie's favourite weapon is her goo shrinker. One blast of slime will shrink her enemies down to size. However, Jessie had better be careful where she points it – Rex couldn't bear it if she made his arms any smaller!

GAME FILE

OCCUPATION: Cowgirl toy

LIKES: Action, adventure, a certain space ranger

DISLIKES: Sitting around doing nothing, being abandoned

SECRET TALENT: Communicating with critters

FAVOURITE GADGET

Goo shrinker

REX

Everyone knows that the tyrannosaurus rex was the scariest of the dinosaurs. Unfortunately poor Rex is more terrified than terrifying. He can't help it – he's just a big green bundle of nerves. Well, wouldn't you be if you had arms this tiny?

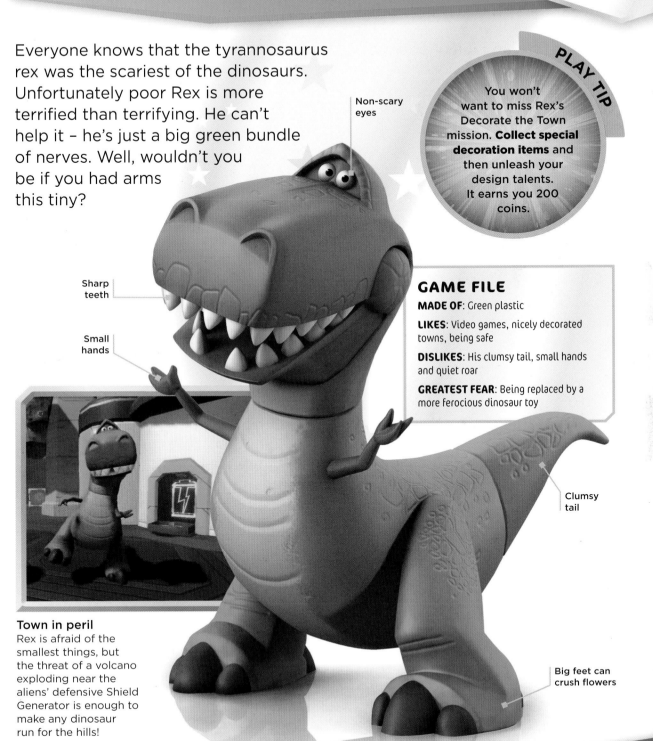

Non-scary eyes

PLAY TIP

You won't want to miss Rex's Decorate the Town mission. **Collect special decoration items** and then unleash your design talents. It earns you 200 coins.

Sharp teeth

Small hands

GAME FILE

MADE OF: Green plastic

LIKES: Video games, nicely decorated towns, being safe

DISLIKES: His clumsy tail, small hands and quiet roar

GREATEST FEAR: Being replaced by a more ferocious dinosaur toy

Clumsy tail

Big feet can crush flowers

Town in peril
Rex is afraid of the smallest things, but the threat of a volcano exploding near the aliens' defensive Shield Generator is enough to make any dinosaur run for the hills!

SPACE ADVENTURE

TO INFINITY AND BEYOND! TOYS TO THE RESCUE

The aliens use this dish to beam distress signals across the galaxy when Zurg attacks them.

Woody has come to save the day!

Buzz and his friends help to repair this tower so that the aliens can create a protective shield around their new planet.

Thanks to Buzz, Woody, Jessie and the gang, this hospital has no new patients. The aliens are unharmed!

STYLISH ALIENS

Life has become a little overcrowded on Pizza Planet, so Buzz and Woody help the aliens to colonise a new planet with more space. The little green guys would like to make a fresh start with a change of style, too. Time to get them to a clothing store so they can each find their own new look.

Space buddies
These aliens can be quite demanding. They really want some new clothes and they want to defeat Zurg. It's going to keep Buzz Lightyear pretty busy.

Pink bow and antenna

Planet logo

Pink alien
This alien has decided that she prefers pink to green.

Classic alien
This little guy sticks with classic space style.

GAME FILE

STYLE DO: Show off your personality with your outfit

STYLE DON'T: Blend in with the crowd

GOLDEN RULE: There are no rules!

PLAY TIP

Unlock the goo shrinker and shoot blobs of purple goo at vehicles and other characters to shrink them. Or, unlock the goo grower and use its green goo to enlarge them.

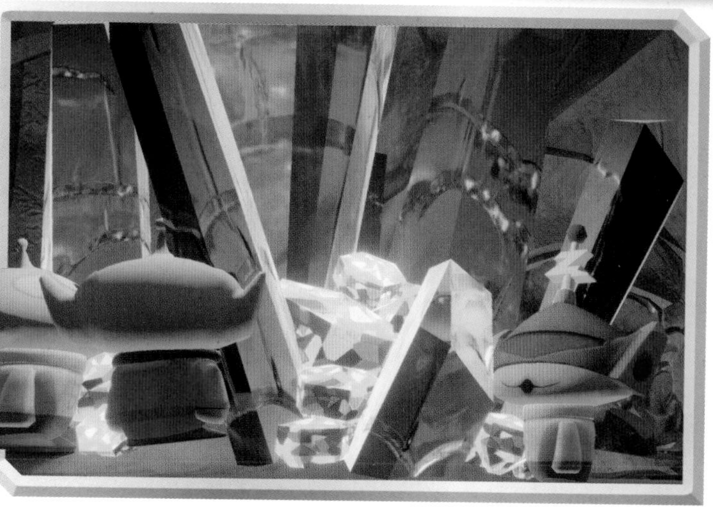

Secret treasure
Things get even more interesting on the new planet when the aliens discover a valuable source of crystals. They must hide it from Zurg!

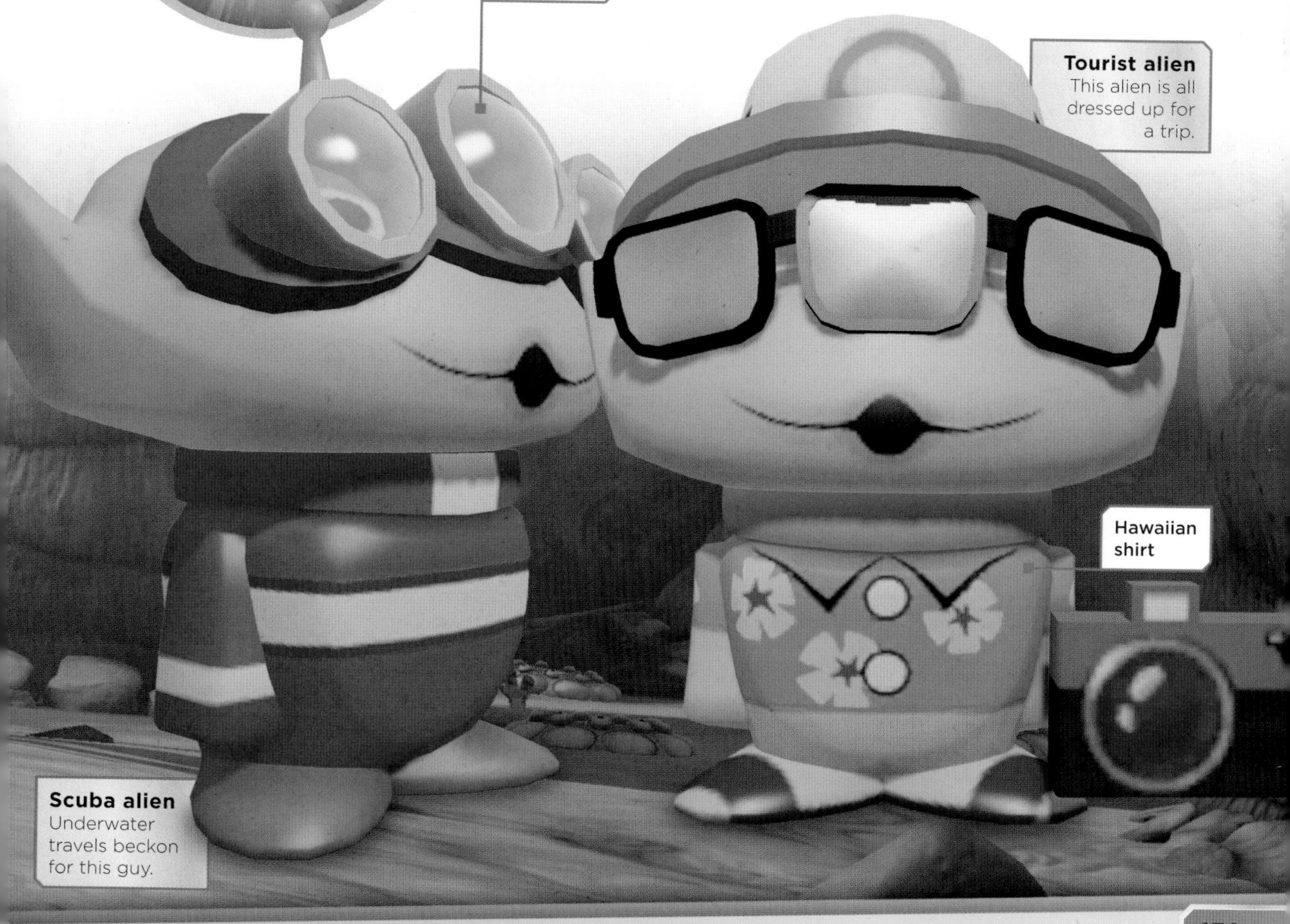

Three-lens goggles
Tourist alien
This alien is all dressed up for a trip.
Hawaiian shirt
Scuba alien
Underwater travels beckon for this guy.

BULLSEYE

Every cowboy needs a trusty steed to ride, and Sheriff Woody's is the best – Bullseye. Woody can always rely on good old Bullseye to be fast, brave and incredibly loyal. His four-legged friend has carried him safely through many adventures, even in space!

Dark brown mane

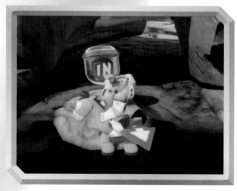

Hoofing around
Bullseye is sweet and loving and extremely friendly. Sheriff Woody is his favourite, but he is happy to have Buzz Lightyear on his back, too. As long as he can gallop faster than the wind, Bullseye is content.

GAME FILE

OCCUPATION: Toy steed

LIKES: Galloping really fast, hanging out with his pals

DISLIKES: Arguments, trotting slowly

FUN FACT: Bullseye's second favourite toy is Jessie. They spent many years stuck in a toy collector's apartment together.

Squishy nose

Western-style saddle

PLAY TIP

Complete **12 Play Set missions** to unlock Bullseye. After purchasing the loyal steed, you will unlock three more exciting challenges.

HAMM

Hamm is probably the cleverest toy in Woody's gang, and he knows it. He can seem downbeat and maybe a bit too honest, but Hamm prefers to think of himself as a realist. The world can be a tough place for a group of toys, so they'd better wise up.

Natural leader
Taking charge comes naturally to a clever pig like Hamm. With his brains, he is great at planning and research. He is the ideal toy to organise a getaway or lead a mission to build a space station.

GAME FILE

OCCUPATION: Piggy bank

PERSONALITY TYPE: Clever, maybe a bit of a know-it-all

LIKES: Reading, playing cards, knowing more than everyone else

DISLIKES: Rushing into an adventure without proper planning

Coin slot

Large nose

PLAY TIP

Have a go at Hamm's Volcano missions. Not only will you explore a new terrain but you will also find some really exciting new toys.

Star command blaster
shoots out red laser

BULLSEYE

Sheriff Woody is always happy
to be reunited with his old pal
Bullseye. His faithful steed is
fast, friendly and prepared to
go anywhere – even outer space!

Tail helps
with balance

Speedy
hooves

GOO SHRINKER

One well-aimed splat of purple gunk from the goo shrinker will make any object, being or vehicle several sizes smaller. Jessie can't wait to shrink a few Zurgbots down to size.

Blob of purple goo
ready to be fired

Nozzle of
shrinker

Goo
chamber

Jetpack wings
deployed

STAR COMMAND
BLASTER AND JETPACK

Buzz Lightyear is proud to carry a standard-issue star command blaster and jetpack. The jetpack will take him to infinity and beyond, and the blaster will help him to protect innocent space citizens.

SLINKY DOG

Sometimes Slinky Dog's back half might take a while to catch up with his front half, but he is the kind of pal that any toy would be lucky to have. He is intelligent, faithful and brave – and his stretchy body is pretty handy when someone needs rescuing.

Happy hound
Slinky Dog is a laid-back guy. It takes a lot to make him angry. However, if you pick on one of his friends, you'll see Slinky Dog get really mad!

GAME FILE

OCCUPATION: Canine stretch toy

PERSONALITY: All-round good guy

HOBBIES: Playing draughts

FAVOURITE SPOT: Under the bed

Long, floppy ears

Big, friendly eyes

PLAY TIP

After you return from the Goo Valley missions, **speak to Slinky** on the mainland to receive another set of action-packed adventures.

Stretchy spring body

Wagging tail

EMPEROR ZURG

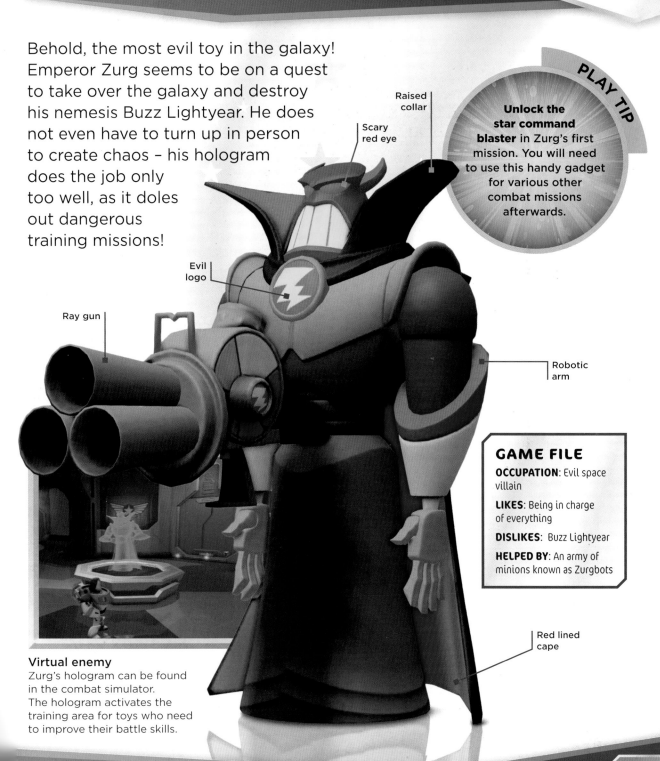

Behold, the most evil toy in the galaxy! Emperor Zurg seems to be on a quest to take over the galaxy and destroy his nemesis Buzz Lightyear. He does not even have to turn up in person to create chaos – his hologram does the job only too well, as it doles out dangerous training missions!

Raised collar

Scary red eye

PLAY TIP

Unlock the star command blaster in Zurg's first mission. You will need to use this handy gadget for various other combat missions afterwards.

Evil logo

Ray gun

Robotic arm

GAME FILE

OCCUPATION: Evil space villain

LIKES: Being in charge of everything

DISLIKES: Buzz Lightyear

HELPED BY: An army of minions known as Zurgbots

Red lined cape

Virtual enemy
Zurg's hologram can be found in the combat simulator. The hologram activates the training area for toys who need to improve their battle skills.

145

ALIENS IN NEED

Sweet-natured, friendly and peace-loving, all these cute green aliens want to do is live in peace. Unfortunately, Emperor Zurg has decided that taking over their planet is the next part of his evil plan. Who will save these toys from Zurg?

GAME FILE

DISTINGUISHING FEATURES: Three eyes and green skin

LIVE: In space on a really cool planet

IN NEED OF: Friends to rescue them

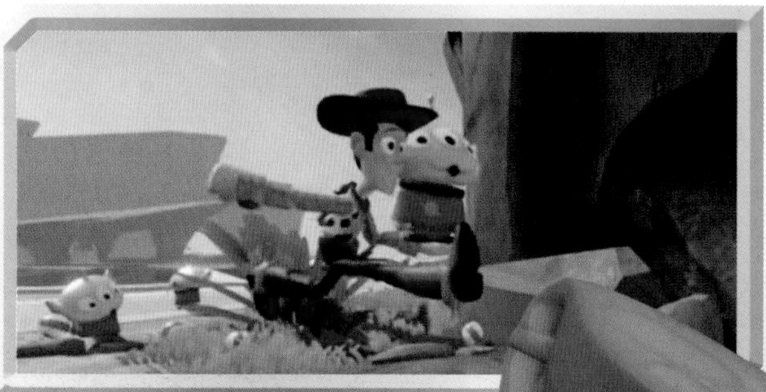

Hero friends
Fortunately the green aliens have some brave friends: Woody, Buzz and the gang won't stand by and watch Zurg hurt their alien pals. They're coming to the rescue!

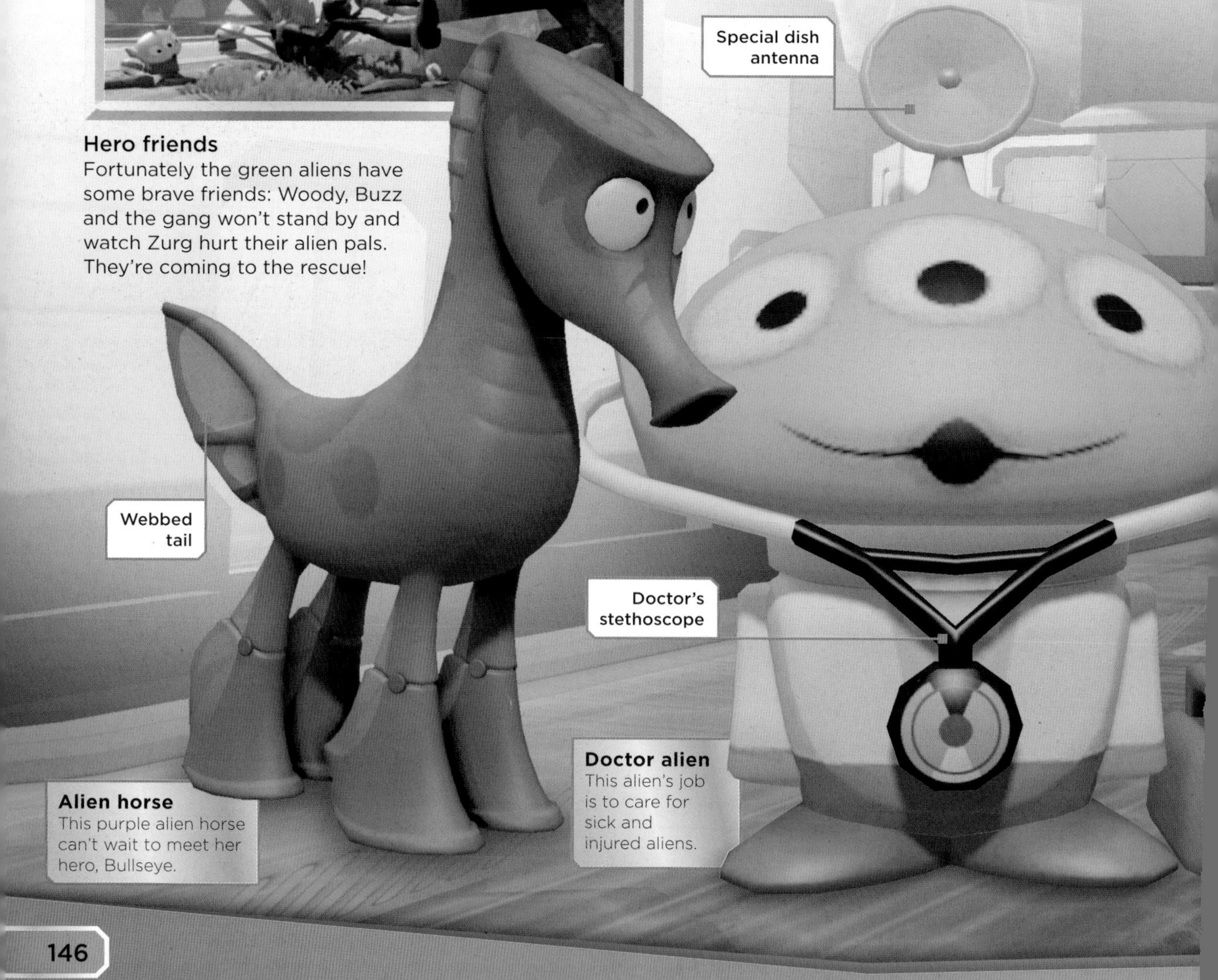

Special dish antenna
Webbed tail
Doctor's stethoscope

Alien horse
This purple alien horse can't wait to meet her hero, Bullseye.

Doctor alien
This alien's job is to care for sick and injured aliens.

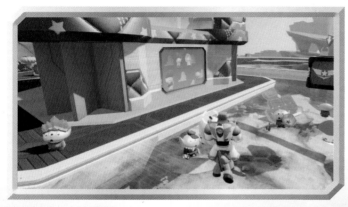

Working together

The aliens are happy that their friends have come to save them. They will help them in any way they can. Together, they will definitely be strong enough to defeat Zurg and his minions.

PLAY TIP

Don't forget to **unlock the jetpack and rocket booster** before taking on the Buzz Lightyear Alien missions. These will make it a lot easier to complete the missions.

Purple antennae

Stylish visor

Tool belt with spanner

Maintenance alien
When things break, the maintenance alien will fix them.

Guard alien
Most guards aren't as stylish as this trendy alien!

TOY BOX
TAKING CHARGE

Jessie is a fun-loving toy, but when her friends get a little too rowdy she's the one who has to tell them to simmer down. Wreck-It Ralph, Sulley and Mr Incredible have trampled all over one of the alien's prize-winning flowerbeds during a game of soccer.

Wreck-It Ralph doesn't always know his own strength!

Jessie tells her pals straight – they need to apologise.

PLAY TIP

In Jessie's Critter Corral Adventure, **use Bullseye to speed things up**. You only have four minutes to gather as many critters as you can.

Sulley is very sorry about the squashed flowers.

Mr Incredible is sulking. He hates being reprimanded.

Jessie has saved the surviving flowers and replanted them in Luigi's spare tyres.

The female alien is grateful for Jessie's help.

MISSION
Somethin' to Prove
MISSION GIVER Slinky Dog

This riding mission is deceptively simple. Buzz must ride Bullseye in a straight line to collect two crates. However, Buzz will have to be quick – there's a 45-second time limit.

1 Use a compass to ride east of the Shield Generator. Find the crate and take it back to the green target zone.

MISSION
Enter the Simulator
MISSION GIVER Slinky Dog

Even an experienced space ranger like Buzz needs to practise his combat skills from time to time. After Buzz buys the combat simulator, Slinky Dog will show him how to use it.

1 Run as fast as you can to the new combat simulator and take the lift to the depths of the building.

MISSION You Floor Me
MISSION GIVER Slinky Dog

When Buzz has unlocked lots of new buildings in the crate crashing missions, he will need to expand the alien village's ground space so there is somewhere for the structures to go.

1 Buzz's goal is to assemble more floor pods. Start by finding the Construct-O-Lot machine's battery.

2

The second crate is west, towards the alien
village. Grab it and then ride Bullseye back
to place the crate in the green zone.

100
CRYSTALS
EARNED

2

Collect training items by finding the Buzz Lightyear
chest over on the right. Leap onto the crates, and
do a double jump to grab the floating green capsule.

25
CRYSTALS
EARNED

2

Leap up the staircase of moving floor panels and ride
them until you find a stationary one. Continue your trek
up to the top until you find a big red button!

100
CRYSTALS
EARNED

DISNEY FRIENDS

What do you get when you mix up a mouse, some princesses, a platypus, a skeleton and a whole bunch of other fun characters? A fantastic adventure, that's what!

CONTENTS

JACK SKELLINGTON

Jack Skellington is the king of Halloween hoaxes, pranks, tricks and stunts. He loves to scare and spook other people. However, if someone turns the tables on the mischievous bag of bones, he can't handle it!

GAME FILE

NICKNAME: The Pumpkin King

LOOKS: Stylish bag o' bones

LIKES: Causing mayhem

DISLIKES: Being the victim of a hoax

FAVOURITE GADGET

Jack-o'-lantern

Stylish striped suit

Bony hand

Fun with friends
Jack is always happy to find a partner in crime. Sulley loves pranking almost as much as Jack. Together the unlikely duo can create some top class mayhem.

Long, scrawny legs

PLAY TIP

Jack's punches do not pack much power. Instead, use his **screaming and screeching techniques** to ward off opponents.

Sensible shoes

Pumpkin power
Jack has developed the ideal weapon for Halloween – jack-o'-lanterns. They look great and share his name!

RAPUNZEL

She has spent most of her life locked in a tower, so it's not surprising that Rapunzel has lots of time for her hobbies – and brushing her very long hair. She's a true dreamer who is brave, honest and kind.

Flower hair decoration

PLAY TIP

Win yourself a gold medal by **collecting 70 lanterns in three minutes** in Rapunzel's Rail Ride Adventure. If you don't quite make it, 50 will still earn you a silver.

Plaited hair style

Simple purple dress

Favourite weapon
Rapunzel has been longing for adventure all her life, and now she has found some. However, she takes a weapon with her – her trusty frying pan!

Bare feet

WRECK-IT RALPH

Thanks to his huge hands and big feet, Ralph has a natural talent for smashing things. For years he used his skills as the bad guy in the Fix-It Felix Jr. video arcade game. However, these days Ralph is exploring his good guy side.

GAME FILE

HEIGHT: 2.7 m (9 ft)

WEIGHT: 292 kg (643 lb)

WANTS TO BE: A hero

HOBBIES: Wrecking, smashing

FAVOURITE GADGET

Cherry bomb

Tough guy
Ralph is so big that even Sulley looks like a teddy bear in comparison. However, he is still good at running away quickly from giant burning hoops and swinging hammers in obstacle courses!

Trademark checked shirt

Huge fist

Shabby dungarees

PLAY TIP

Scatter your foes with one of Ralph's cherry bombs. Boom! Now even the mightiest of your opponents will be shaking in their shoes.

VANELLOPE VON SCHWEETZ

Vanellope Von Schweetz was a princess in her racing video game, and now she is the president! She used to be a computer glitch which made her an outsider, but she learnt to love her teleporting powers and her glitch is now her strongest asset.

Ribbon keeps hair out of the way

GAME FILE

OCCUPATION: Former video game princess

LIKES: Driving fast, winning

DISLIKES: Losing

FAVORITE GADGETS

Candy cart   Cherry bomb

Burning rubber
Vanellope is sweet and kind, but she is also super competitive, especially when she is driving her candy cart. She is determined to win every race she enters, and some giant monster truck wheels are just the tool she needs!

Candy hair jewels

PLAY TIP
Vanellope's candy cart can be unlocked if you **open her treasure chest**. When you've unlocked it, listen to race music from the *Sugar Rush* video game while you take it for a spin.

Mismatched striped socks

Explosive personality
Like her friend Ralph, Vanellope likes to stun her opponents with a cherry bomb. If she doesn't beat them with speed, her cherry bomb blast should do the trick!

TOY BOX
MIXED-UP MAYHEM

When characters team up with the coolest vehicles from their worlds, it makes for some spectacular adventures. Sometimes the unlikeliest pairs make a terrific team – Jack Skellington and a Cinderella look-alike are winning co-drivers in this race.

The Cozy Cone Motel is the perfect spot to relax and unwind after the race.

Luigi's famous tyre shop is on hand, in case anyone has a blow out.

This Cinderella look-alike thinks Jack is fun and not at all spooky.

Jack drives the Astro Space Blaster cruiser scarily fast!

Hangin' Ten Stitch and Mr Incredible prove that an alien and a Super make a great surfing team.

Woody has swapped hooves for wheels, and he loves it!

TOY BOX

Take part in various Mastery Adventures in the Toy Box mode. **You will learn interesting tips and tricks** on how to build and manoeuvre your Toy Box.

ANNA

Warm-hearted and friendly, Anna is the perfect little sister. She adores her older sister, Elsa, and can't understand why she keeps her distance. Anna is determined to get close to Elsa – Elsa is her sister and Anna will love her no matter what.

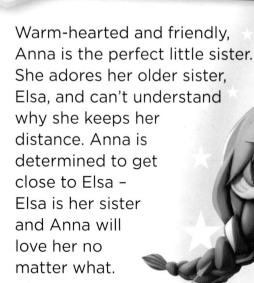

Adventurous Anna
Anna is courageous and determined. She would face any danger to keep her family and friends safe. Of course it's nice if she has help – although Ralph may cause an avalanche...

Light brown hair with ice-white stripe

Rope for climbing obstacles

GAME FILE

OCCUPATION: Princess

PERSONALITY TYPE: Fun, open and caring

LIVES: The kingdom of Arendelle

MOST LIKELY TO: Make friends and help people

FAVOURITE GADGETS

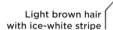

Shovel swing

Climbing hook

Pretty floral pattern

PLAY TIP

Use the **rocket booster** in Anna's Chilling Challenge to soar up to the top tier and collect high-value objects. But don't go so high that you can't see the objects anymore!

Embroidered boots

ELSA

On the outside, Elsa looks like the perfect queen, but she also has a special power – she can create ice and snow. However, Elsa can't always control her gifts, so she prefers to hide away in case she accidentally hurts someone.

Ice-blonde hair

Powerful fingers

Ice to see you
Sometimes Elsa does manage to control her icy powers. She creates freezing balls of ice to launch at her enemies. A direct hit and the villains are knocked out cold!

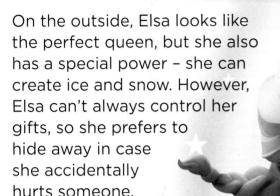

Taking control
With a little help from her sister, Elsa realises that she can't hide away forever. Besides, she's missing out on too many fun adventures! Flying a helicopter is such fun and so is catching bad guys like Syndrome.

Pale blue gown

PLAY TIP

Put Elsa's skills to the test in Elsa's Slingshot Gallery. Hit as many objects as possible to **collect extra points** before the time runs out.

Shoes match her dress

GAME FILE

OCCUPATION: Queen

PERSONALITY TYPE:
Serious and shy

FAVOURITE PERSON: Her little sister, Anna

WORRIES ABOUT: Accidentally freezing people, especially Anna

FAVOURITE GADGET

Freeze ball

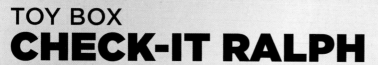

TOY BOX
CHECK-IT RALPH

Wreck-It Ralph has worked hard to prove that he is not just an arcade-game bad guy. He has made lots of new friends and taken up some new, non-destructive hobbies. He is even learning to play chess, but he's not very good!

Chess games always start with a move from a small piece, known as a pawn. This soldier of hearts is excited to begin this game!

Maximus makes the perfect white knight chess piece. He is brave and loyal.

This Agrabah Guard is a rook. He can move horizontally or vertically across any number of squares.

Gather as many collectibles as you can in Ralph's Wreck and Wrangle Adventure. It's a tricky challenge and you only have six minutes to complete it.

Tia Dalma has a new role – as the queen. She likes being the most powerful chess piece!

Playing chess requires patience, tactical thinking and a lot of practice. At least using the magic wand to move the pieces is fun!

PHINEAS FLYNN

He might only be a kid, but Phineas Flynn is already a genius inventor. He likes to invent things that will make his life easier and more fun. His new water slide will not only take him anywhere he wants to go, it's an awesome ride, too.

Large, clever eyes

Croquet anyone!
Like most kids, Phineas loves playing games. However, he always likes to add his own twist to regular sports – this flamingo mallet should liven up a game of croquet!

Messy red hair

Strike!
Another of Phineas' cool inventions is this baseball shooter. It is the perfect way to scatter his enemies, and practise his pitching.

Cheerful smile

PLAY TIP
Explore Phineas' five character chests and unlock a wealth of exciting goodies, including a Candace costume and the baseball shooter.

GAME FILE
OCCUPATION: Kid/inventor

LIKES: Creating crazy but useful gadgets for family and friends

DISLIKES: Being told off by his sister Candace

FAVOURITE GADGETS

Water slide   Baseball shooter

AGENT P

Perry the platypus lives an amazing double life. To Phineas, he is a cute and not-too-smart pet, but when Phineas isn't looking, Perry leaps in to action as a daring government agent. Known by the code name Agent P, Perry's job is to protect the world from the evil Dr. Doofenshmirtz.

GAME FILE

OCCUPATION: Pet and secret agent

SPECIES: Duck-billed platypus

FRIENDS: Phineas and Ferb

ENEMY: Dr Doofenschmirtz

FAVOURITE GADGET

Flying fedora

Trademark fedora hat

Secret missions
Agent P has faced many dangerous situations. He is an expert in dodging obstacles, hand-to-hand combat and climbing up poles at speed.

Agent P doesn't talk with his bright yellow beak – good for playing dumb!

Fists ready for action

Flat platypus tail

PLAY TIP

Agent P's flying fedora is not just a stylish accessory. **Hurl it at enemies** as a defence mechanism, and take them by surprise.

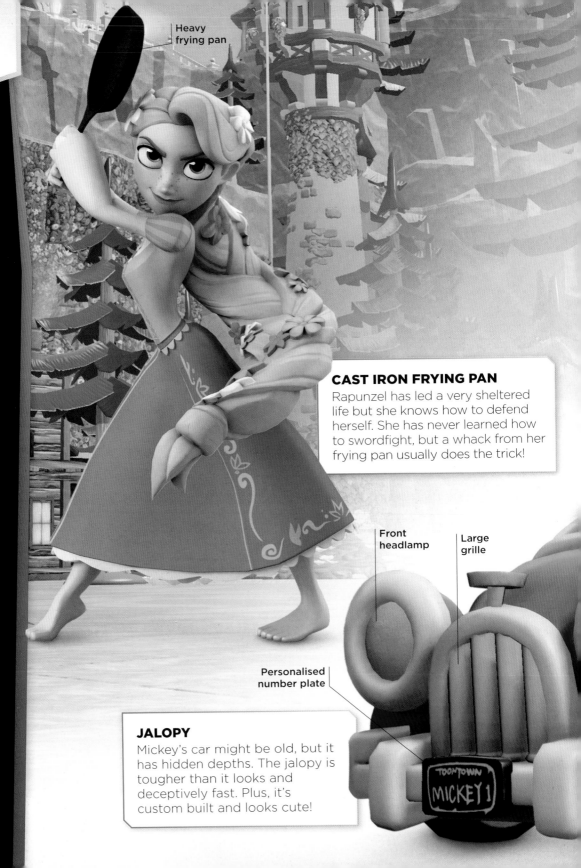

Heavy
frying pan

CAST IRON FRYING PAN

Rapunzel has led a very sheltered life but she knows how to defend herself. She has never learned how to swordfight, but a whack from her frying pan usually does the trick!

Front
headlamp

Large
grille

Personalised
number plate

TOONTOWN
MICKEY 1

JALOPY

Mickey's car might be old, but it has hidden depths. The jalopy is tougher than it looks and deceptively fast. Plus, it's custom built and looks cute!

Jack-o'-lantern
ready to explode

Jack takes aim
for a big throw
at his target.

JACK-O'-LANTERNS
Jack Skellington's trademark
exploding jack-o'-lanterns
usually keep foes at bay.
They also make useful, if
a little freaky, nightlights!

Shiny red
paintwork

Rear bumper
softens hard
knocks

CANDY CART

Steering
wheel

Multicoloured and very
fast, the candy cart
suits Vanellope Von
Schweetz perfectly.

BASEBALL SHOOTER

Release
switch

Phineas invented this
useful weapon, which
can shoot baseballs
faster than any pitcher.

SHOVEL SWING

Easy-
grip
handle

This weapon is fit for
a princess – and it's
great for digging, too.
Anna carries it
wherever
she goes.

SORCERER'S APPRENTICE
MICKEY

Fun-loving and fearless, this famous mouse needs no introduction. Everyone loves Sorcerer's Apprentice Mickey – he always has plenty of offers for new friends. He's ready to face any adventure with optimism, enthusiasm and a little magic.

Car pool
Mickey can't resist trying out Mr Incredible's cool sports car. It may be super fast, but Mickey still prefers his good old, reliable jalopy.

Pointed sorcerer's hat

GAME FILE

OCCUPATION:
Sorcerer's apprentice

MASTER: Sorcerer Yen Sid

PERSONALITY TYPE:
Fun, fun, fun

FAVOURITE GADGETS

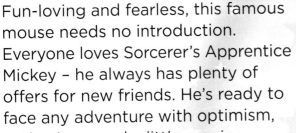

Broom   Jalopy

Trademark mouse ears

Long red robes

New pals
Mickey is off on an adventure with some new friends. Lightning McQueen and Jack Sparrow are no slouches, but they'll have a tough time keeping up with Mickey!

PLAY TIP

Taking part in Mickey's Magical Escape Adventure is a great way to win medals and improve your score. **Complete it in as little time as possible** for maximum points.

Tan shoes

DONALD DUCK

Most of the time, Donald is a pretty easy-going duck. He loves relaxing and just taking life easy. He's happiest hanging out with his best pal, Mickey. However, life isn't always picture perfect. When things go wrong, Donald can go from relaxed to raging in seconds.

Jaunty blue sailor's hat

Angry expression

Show-off
Sometimes, Donald Duck can't resist showing off a little, even taking centre stage in a glitzy parade. He wishes his pal Mickey could see him!

Yellow, webbed feet

GAME FILE

APPEARANCE: Blue sailor outfit and red bow tie

PERSONALITY: Changeable – gets mad easily

BEST FRIEND: Sorcerer's Apprentice Mickey

TOP SECRET: Donald's middle name is Fauntleroy.

Hammer time
When Donald gets mad, he loves smashing things with his hammer. It makes him feel so much better! He also enjoys throwing things.

TOY BOX
UP, UP AND AWAY!

Aladdin and Jasmine love exploring faraway places, and for them, there is only one way to travel – on a magic carpet! It's fast, environmentally friendly and has amazing views. The adventurous pair make new friends along the way, too.

Agent P is not a fan of carpet travel and he wishes Phineas had put in seatbelts.

Phineas' custom-made magic carpet has a sofa and a TV.

PLAY TIP

Give Aladdin a makeover by using his costume Power Disc, Rags to Riches. See him transform into a handsome prince wearing royal robes.

The magic carpet takes Aladdin and Jasmine anywhere they want.

Aladdin loves flying. When he sees the cities far below him, he feels like a king!

Magic carpets aren't for everyone. Some people prefer to travel by flying house...

Rapunzel's floating birthday lanterns light up the skies.

Jasmine is so relaxed on the magic carpet that she doesn't even need to hold on.

ALADDIN

Aladdin hasn't had an easy life. As an orphan he has lived on the streets and often had to steal to survive. However, he's not a bad person. He's kind, loyal and very brave. Aladdin just needs a little bit of good fortune.

Fez hat

PLAY TIP

Unleash the power of Aladdin's special attack by **summoning up purple smoke** from his magic lamp that can defeat enemies.

Well-worn waistcoat

Rags to riches
With a little bit of magic, Aladdin can transform himself into handsome Prince Ali. He hopes to win Princess Jasmine's heart, and her hand in marriage.

Ragged trousers

Magic lamp
Finding a magical lamp changed Aladdin's life forever. Not only does the Genie grant his wishes, but Aladdin can also use it as a weapon.

GAME FILE
PERSONALITY: Quick-witted, courageous and generous

WOULD LIKE TO BE:
A rich prince

TOP SECRET: Aladdin doesn't think a street boy would be good enough for Princess Jasmine

JASMINE

Jasmine has been brought up in a luxurious palace with everything she could wish for – fine foods, pretty clothes and even a pet tiger. However, there is one thing she doesn't have: freedom. Jasmine longs to make her own decisions and live her life the way she chooses.

Jewelled hairband

Pale green top

Perfect partners
Flying on magic carpets through Agrabah, Aladdin and Jasmine can finally be what they truly want to be ... together!

PLAY TIP
To take on foes, **enlist Jasmine's special attack,** in which the magic carpet will spiral around at incredible speeds and damage any bad guys nearby.

Newfound freedom
Jasmine has always longed for adventure, and now she's found it. She can ride bikes, defeat her enemies and go wherever her heart desires. Life outside the palace is dangerous, but exciting!

Silk slippers

Matching trousers

AGRABAH GUARD

The kingdom of Agrabah lies deep in the desert. It is protected by hundreds of palace guards, who see their sole duty as protecting the Sultan and his daughter, Princess Jasmine. They are strong, tough and unfortunately, also pretty nasty.

Jewelled motif to show rank

GAME FILE

OCCUPATION: Guarding the Sultan and upholding the laws of the kingdom

PERSONALITY TYPE: Fierce, forceful, stubborn

ENJOYS: Chasing criminals, putting crooks in jail, being scary

ENEMIES: Lawbreakers, especially Aladdin

Teeth knocked out in brawls with crooks

Trouble!
Agrabah is also home to Aladdin. He takes great delight in outsmarting the palace guards. Unfortunately, they also take great delight in chasing him with their curved swords....

PLAY TIP

The Agrabah Guards are a good defensive choice to take on enemies. They travel in packs and are never afraid to outnumber criminals.

Strong legs for chasing down targets

Traditional leather slippers

MERIDA

Sixteen-year-old Merida is a Scottish princess, but she's not interested in princes or pretty dresses. She prefers archery, sword-fighting and exploring. Merida is young and bold, and she can't wait to throw herself headlong into whatever adventures life has in store for her.

GAME FILE

OCCUPATION: Princess

PERSONALITY:
Kind, brave and stubborn

MOST LIKELY TO:
Have a crazy adventure involving a bear

LEAST LIKELY TO:
Go to a ball

New pals
Merida can ride a surfboard almost as well as she can shoot arrows. Jack and Vanellope struggle to catch up and think that the Scottish princess can be a real show-off sometimes.

Distinctive red hair

Plain blue dress

Trusty bow

Protective arm guard

PLAY TIP

Upgrade Merida's aim with elemental freeze arrows. These allow her to freeze her enemies, so she has plenty of time to get a clear shot.

TOY BOX
HIGHLAND GAMES

Merida has decided to give her friends an archery lesson.
Mr Incredible and Buzz are famous for their strength and
bravery, but can they hit a small target when under pressure?
First, Merida will show them how it is done.

PLAY TIP

Be careful
while collecting
cakes for the witch
in Merida's Brave
Toy Box game.
There are bears
hiding everywhere,
just waiting
to attack.

Merida's bow
is taller than
she is.

Mr Incredible doesn't
feel strong or brave
when Merida is firing
arrows near him.

Merida is an
expert archer –
she never misses.

This townsperson
dressed as Merida's
mother, Queen Elinor,
is proud of the Scottish
princess's skills.

Buzz thinks he'd rather face Zurg than Merida's arrows.

This bear lies in wait for any cake.

A Scottish townsperson can't bear to watch.

TINKER BELL

Like all the fairies in Pixie Hollow, Tinker Bell works hard all year round making sure that the seasons happen right on time. Tink's job is to fix broken things, but she is also skilled in magic. Just a little sprinkling of her magical Pixie Dust can heal anyone.

Trademark bun

Delicate wings

GAME FILE

OCCUPATION: Tinker fairy

LIVES: Pixie Hollow, Neverland

POWERS: Flying, healing and general magic

ALWAYS CARRIES: A supply of Pixie Dust and her wand

Green leaf dress

Pom-poms

Brave fairy
Tink is tiny but she is also tough. The little fairy isn't scared of Stitch's blaster gun. She knows she can fly far away before Stitch even has time to react.

PLAY TIP
If you are overwhelmed by tricky opponents, **use Tinker Bell's ability to glide**. She can fly all the way up to the stratosphere, leaving her enemies red-faced.

STITCH

Stitch isn't really so bad, he just has a knack for creating trouble wherever he goes. It's not his fault – he is the result of an alien experiment, so it is understandable that he has a fair few glitches. Aside from having a flair for mischief, he is very intelligent and has super strength. Life is certainly never dull when Stitch is around.

PLAY TIP

Help Stitch cause the most possible damage by unlocking 626's Dual Blaster Attack. This will allow him to **fire from two blasters at the same time**.

Large, floppy ears

Sharp claws

Huge teeth

GAME FILE

PERSONALITY: Complex, mischievous

ABILITIES: Wall climbing and jumping really high

WEAPONS: Two blasters

SIGNATURE MOVE: Curling up into a ball and rolling into enemies

Comfy ride
A flying bed is the perfect vehicle for Stitch and his pal Captain Sparrow. From up here, this trouble-loving pair can create even more chaos.

HIRO

Hiro Hamada was an ordinary teenager, albeit a super-bright one, until his he lost his brother in a mysterious fire. With his life turned upside down, Hiro decided to use his brainpower to keep other people safe. He created a high-tech super hero team – Big Hero 6!

GAME FILE

AGE: 14

OCCUPATION: Student and super hero

ABILITIES: Genius-level intelligence

WEARS: A special super suit

Protective helmet

Kevlar-armoured gauntlet

Hiro's new mission
Whether he's fighting alongside his five super hero friends or flying solo, Hiro has pledged to make his city a safe place to live.

Microbots!
Hiro used his genius to invent tiny robots called microbots. These join together to make all kinds of shapes. Hiro can use them to battle enemies or climb on top of things.

Magnetic knee pad (to attach to Baymax)

High-tech trainers

PLAY TIP

Avoid danger with Hiro's handy booster jumps. His swarms of microbots are also incredibly useful – he can control tens of thousands of them!

BAYMAX

Baymax was constructed by Hiro's brother, Tadashi. He was originally built as a healthcare companion to treat the sick and injured. Later, Hiro modified the giant robot into a warrior and invited him to join the Big Hero 6 team.

PLAY TIP

Take advantage of Baymax's ability to karate chop opponents, as well as to blast multiple enemies with his charged rocket fists.

Wings designed for high speeds

Hiro can ride on Baymax's back.

Access port for computer chips

Protective shoulder plates

Rocket fist weapon

GAME FILE

OCCUPATION: Protector, hero, healthcare companion

AFFILIATION: Big Hero 6

BEST FRIEND: Hiro Hamada

WOULD DO: Anything to protect Hiro

Boosters built into legs

Upgraded companion
Baymax's original job was to keep people safe and healthy. Hiro altered his programming to add strength and flying skills, and upgraded him with armour!

TOY BOX
OUTNUMBERED

Hiro and Baymax like a challenge, but it doesn't take a genius to work out they are outnumbered. However, with Hiro's brains and Baymax's brawn, this ragtag band of pirates, outlaws and palace guards doesn't stand a chance!

Hammerhead? Baymax is about to give Maccus a real headache!

The sneaky Agrabah guard thinks a surprise attack from behind is a good idea.

This turtle-headed sea rogue should have stayed in his shell.

Baymax is not only huge and strong, he will also protect Hiro in any way he can.

PLAY TIP

Hiro and Baymax make a great team. Use their Honey Lemon's Ice Capsules Power Disc **to freeze your enemies** in a cloud of frost.

Hiro won't lose this fight. He has youth, brains, and Baymax on his side.

This outlaw isn't welcome in Colby and he's not welcome here either.

CHARACTER GALLERY

In the Disney Infinity universe, you will meet some special characters. Some will be brave heroes with important missions to undertake, while others will be wicked villains, doing everything to stop them. Watch out for a host of crazy, fun-loving folk along the way, too.

Captain Jack Sparrow
Playable

Barbossa
Playable

Davy Jones
Playable

THE INCREDIBLES

Mr Incredible
Playable

Mrs Incredible
Playable

Dash Incredible
Playable

Violet Incredible
Playable

Syndrome
Playable

Rick Dicker
Non-playable

Edna Mode
Non-playable

Student
Non-playable

Working mum
Non-playable

Maintenance man
Non-playable

Businessman
Non-playable

MONSTERS UNIVERSITY

Sulley
Playable

Mike
Playable

Art
Non-playable

Terri & Terry
Non-playable

Archie
Non-playable

Don Carlton
Non-playable

Red winged monster
Non-playable

Yellow monster
Non-playable

Blue striped monster
Non-playable

Maccus

Non-playable

Gibbs

Non-playable

Tia Dalma

Non-playable

Pintel

Non-playable

Ragetti

Non-playable

Driftwood

Non-playable

Clam

Non-playable

Mirage

Non-playable

Omnidroid #1

Non-playable

Omnidroid #2

Non-playable

Omnidroid #3

Non-playable

Hardworking teacher

Non-playable

Randy

Playable

Squishy

Non-playable

Big brawny beast

Non-playable

Hoops dude

Non-playable

Student patrol

Non-playable

Scared Scarer

Non-playable

Patrol buddy

Non-playable

Light blue monster

Non-playable

Purple monster

Non-playable

CARS

Lightning McQueen

Playable

Mater

Playable

Guido

Non-playable

Fillmore
Non-playable

Luigi
Non-playable

Holley Shiftwell
Playable

Francesco
Playable

Chick Hicks
Non-playable

Butch Cavendish
Non-playable

Red Harrington
Non-playable

Shotgun man
Non-playable

Pistol man
Non-playable

TNT man
Non-playable

Sheriff
Non-playable

Train Engineer
Non-playable

Tourist alien
Non-playable

Bullseye
Non-playable

Hamm
Non-playable

Slinky Dog
Non-playable

Emperor Zurg
Non-playable

Alien horse
Non-playable

Vanellope Von Schweetz
Playable

Anna
Playable

Elsa
Playable

Phineas Flynn
Playable

Agent P
Playable

Sorcerer's Apprentice Mickey
Playable

Donald Duck
Playable

Aladdin
Playable

Ramone
Non-playable

Flo
Non-playable

Finn
Non-playable

THE LONE RANGER

The Lone Ranger
Playable

Tonto
Playable

TOY STORY

Woody
Playable

Buzz Lightyear
Playable

Jessie
Playable

Rex
Non-playable

Pink alien
Non-playable

Classic alien
Non-playable

Scuba alien
Non-playable

Doctor alien
Non-playable

Maintenance alien
Non-playable

Guard alien
Non-playable

DISNEY FRIENDS

Jack Skellington
Playable

Rapunzel
Playable

Wreck-It Ralph
Playable

Jasmine
Playable

Agrabah Guard
Non-playable

Merida
Playable

Tinker Bell
Playable

Stitch
Playable

Hiro
Playable

Baymax
Playable

INDEX

COMPATIBILITY CHART		DISNEY INFINITY	DISNEY INFINITY 2.0
Disney INFINITY	DISNEY INFINITY FIGURES	✓	✓
	DISNEY INFINITY PLAY SET PIECES	✓	✗
	DISNEY INFINITY POWER DISCS	✓	✓
Disney INFINITY 2.0	DISNEY INFINITY 2.0 FIGURES	✗	✓
	DISNEY INFINITY 2.0 PLAY SET PIECES	✗	✓
	DISNEY INFINITY 2.0 POWER DISCS	✗	✓
	DISNEY INFINITY 2.0 TOY BOX GAMES DISCS	✗	✓

Penguin Random House

Senior Editor Scarlett O'Hara
Senior Art Editors Clive Savage, Lisa Robb
Project Editor Lisa Stock
Editors Ruth Amos, David Fentiman, Gaurav Joshi
Assistant Art Editors Pranika Jain, Akansha Jain
Producer, Pre-Production Siu Yin Chan
Producer Alex Bell
Pre-Production Manager Sunil Sharma
DTP Designers Umesh Singh Rawat, Rajdeep Singh
Managing Editors Laura Gilbert, Chitra Subramanyam
Managing Art Editors Maxine Pedliham, Neha Ahuja
Art Director Lisa Lanzarini
Publisher Julie Ferris
Publishing Director Simon Beecroft

DK would like to thank Chelsea Alon, Brittany Candau, Scott Piehl, Rachel Alor
and Daniel Saeva at Disney Publishing; and Kristie Crawford, Alissa Newton,
Stephanie Martinelli and Yolande Vandenbulcke at Disney Interactive.

First published in Great Britain in 2014 by
Dorling Kindersley Limited
80 Strand, London WC2R 0RL
A Penguin Random House Company

10 9 8 7 6 5 4 3 2 1

001–259443–Feb/15

Page design copyright © 2015 Dorling Kindersley Limited.

A CIP catalogue record for this book
is available from the British Library.

ISBN: 978-0-24100-845-4

Colour reproduction by Alta Image Ltd, UK
Printed and bound in China by Hung Hing

Some character and story details are based on the movies
and not on the Disney Infinity video game.

A WORLD OF IDEAS:
SEE ALL THERE IS TO KNOW